Psychic Dreaming

Craig Hamilton-Parker

*Illustrated by Steinar Lund
and Lynne Milton*

STERLING PUBLISHING CO., Ii
New York

This book is dedicated to my wife, Jane,
and to all those who have
the courage to follow their dreams.

Library of Congress Cataloging-in-Publication Data Available

2 4 6 8 10 9 7 5 3 1

Published by Sterling Publishing Co., Inc.
387 Park Avenue South, New York, NY 10016
© 2004 by Craig Hamilton-Parker
Distributed in Canada by Sterling Publishing
c/o Canadian Manda Group, One Atlantic Avenue, Suite 105
Toronto, Ontario, Canada M6K 3E7
Distributed in Great Britain by Chrysalis Books Group PLC
The Chrysalis Building, Bramley Road, London W10 6SP, England
Distributed in Australia by Capricorn Link (Australia) Pty. Ltd.
P.O. Box 704, Windsor, NSW 2756, Australia

Manufactured in China
All rights reserved

Sterling ISBN: 1-4027-0474-7

All that we see or seem
Is but a dream within a dream.

EDGAR ALLAN POE, POET

Contents

How to Use This Book 6

Introduction 7

Accidents 10

Afterlife 11

Animal Psychics 15

Animal Spirits 16

Animal Symbols 18

Banal Psychic Dreams 21

Biblical Prophecies 22

Birth 24

Buildings and Places 25

Clairvoyance 27

Coincidence and
  Synchronicity 29

Crystals 30

Death and Dying 31

Disasters 34

Dream Incubation (Seeding) 37

Extra Sensory Perception (ESP) 39

Future 40

Guides and Gurus 40

Health and Healing 43

Hypnagogic and
  Hypnopompic Dreams 45

Intuition 47

Journeys 48

Lucid Dreams 52

Luck 53

Money 57

Mutual Dreams 61

Nature 61

Numerology 65

Numinous Dreams
  (Grand Dreams) 67

Omens 69

Oneiromancy 70

Oracles 71

Contents

Oriental Dreams 76

Out-of-Body Experiences
   (OBEs) 79

Paralysis 81

Parapsychology 83

Past Lives 84

People 86

Precognition 87

Prediction 87

Prophecy 88

Protection 90

Psychic Attacks 91

Psychokinesis 93

Remote Viewing (RV) 94

Serialism 95

Skepticism 96

Soulmates 97

Spells 99

Success 100

Superstition 102

Symbolism 103

Telepathy 107

Time 109

Tribal Dream Interpretation 111

Unidentified Flying Objects
   (UFOs) 115

Unconscious Mind 118

Universal Mind 118

Wicca and Witchcraft 120

Work 123

World Events 124

Xenoglossy 127

Yoga Traditions 128

Zodiac 132

Bibliography 133

Index of Psychic Dream
   Meanings 136

About the Author 144

How to Use This Book

This book is a directory of psychic dreams. It includes short essays about the different forms of psychic dreams as well as examples and true stories. You can read this book from cover to cover, starting at the beginning, or you can dip into specific sections when you want to get insight into a particular dream theme. Common psychic dream symbols are highlighted in bold type. The back of the book includes an index of dream themes which you can use to look up the entries for the hundreds of specific psychic dream symbols mentioned in the text.

Introduction

Trust in dreams, for in them is hidden the gate to eternity.
KAHLIL GIBRAN, LEBANESE POET

As a psychic-medium for over 20 years, I am not surprised when dreams tell the future or connect us to other places or people. For me, psychic powers are self-evident. I experience them in my work when I communicate with the dead or demonstrate psychic and prophetic powers before an audience. My wife is also a medium. It is not uncommon for us to share dreams and to experience telepathy during normal waking life. I blew up like a balloon when Jane was pregnant, and she knows when I am in danger or distress. If she beams me a shopping list when I go out, I invariably return with obscure items she forgot to mention before I left. In our family, psychic power is part of everyday life.

I believe that this power exists in all of us and can be discovered by anyone who seeks to find it. One of the richest areas of psychic power is our dreams.

I always meditate before doing psychic or mediumistic work. Without this period of attunement, my abilities are much less active, and my demonstrations and consultations may be a struggle. For me, and for most true psychic-mediums, meditation is essential for the successful use of ESP gifts. Since the dream state is a highly relaxed condition, dreams connect with the same relaxed inner states that are discovered during meditation. Dreams are a productive place for psychic experiences. Parapsychologists agree. They have found that a degree of relaxation is necessary for success in their laboratory experiments. Deep relaxation helps to minimize interference from conscious thoughts and allows the intuition to become dominant.

A great many people who make no claim to having psychic powers in waking life discover that their sixth sense awakens when they dream. The extensive experiments made between 1930 and 1960 by Dr. Louisa Rhine, the wife of the famous parapsychologist Joseph Banks Rhine, evaluated over 10,000 cases of spontaneous psychic events. She found that over half of them occurred during dreams. Most of these psychic dreams were about future events. They included everything from the tragic to the banal. Often these psychic dreams related to loved ones, but sometimes they were about complete strangers.

Clearly, sleep is an altered state that everyone experiences. It is an easy way to make your own fascinating study into the paranormal. In one study of 290 random dream reports, researchers found that 38 of

Psychic dreams can guide you through the labyrinth of your inner being.

them—8.8 percent—could be classified as paranormal to some extent or other. Psychic dreams are commonplace yet intriguing. I am sure that everyone who wants to can discover the psychic side of dreams. Psychic dreams can also be of tremendous help to avoid pitfalls and discover new ways to find good fortune. Most importantly, they give you a glimpse into yourself and your own extraordinary potential. Psychic dreams may even save your life.

When working with psychic dreams, in particular those that appear to tell the future, you need to keep your feet on the ground. Remember that dreams speak in symbols. Sometimes, these symbols represent events in the real world and even prophecies about the future. However, most dreams express the way you feel and reflect your fears and worries. If you dream about a **car crash** or an **accident**, it's probably not a prediction. These are classic symbols that your life is out of control and you're in danger of an emotional crash. Similarly, many people fear they are about to die if they dream about **death**. Such a dream may symbolize an underused part of your personality or the end of one phase of your life so another can begin. Throughout this book, you'll find explanations of symbolism to help you recognize the difference between psychic dreams and those expressing fear.

No dream about the future represents absolute certainty. Dreams deal with probability and with likelihood because the future is not set in stone. We have free will to choose our way ahead. Psychic dreams are not an excuse to abdicate responsibility or bemoan fate. Psychic dreams give insight into potential pitfalls and offer signposts on the way to good fortune; they do not tell the future. We are responsible for our future because of the choices we make today.

Most dreams are filled with what Freud called *Tagesreste*, the residue of jobs, relationships, and other things that influence life and cause worry. But there are also instances when dreams touch the same worlds our ancestors knew—a world of gods, deities, demons, and angels, where the familiar world we know disappears. These dreams transcend the banal world of ordinary life and lead through the inner labyrinth to the very heart of our being. Psychic dreams put us in touch with the center of the soul, giving insight into the twists and turns of life and empowering us to take charge of our destiny and create a brighter future.

ACCIDENTS

When all is said, melancholy is the mother of dream, and of all terrors of the night whatsoever.

THOMAS NASH, BRITISH AUTHOR

Accident dreams are rarely what they seem and are more likely to allude to personal issues than actual events in the future. Nonetheless, dreams often give practical warnings, so approach them logically and try to assess your feelings during the dream and when you wake up. The subconscious is aware of things that the waking mind may be too busy (or emotionally unable) to register. For example, you may not consciously notice a dangerous broken banister, but the subconscious may give you a dream about falling down the stairs in order to bring the danger to your attention. Discovering that the dream was right about the banister is not necessarily paranormal but a subconsciously observed fact.

Dreams about accidents are not necessarily a premonition of the future. These nightmares may reveal deep anxieties and fears. A car crash may represent your emotional state. Are you are driving yourself too hard? Perhaps you need to slow down a bit. Do you feel as if your emotions are being crushed? Have you recently experienced a shock or had news that is disastrous to your security?

Dreams about accidents happening to other people may indicate your hidden resentment toward them. Are you jealous perhaps, and do you begrudge them their success? Unexpressed jealousy, resentment, and hatred often find a release through dreams.

Dreams rarely reveal an unalterable fate. If your dreams gave you unrestricted access to the future, you might learn things you wouldn't want to know about yourself and other people, such as deaths and accidents about to happen. With complete ESP, it wouldn't be possible to wall off all the pain and suffering in the world or distinguish between your own thoughts and other people's. ESP during psychic dreaming may be limited to what we can cope with; otherwise, we'd never sleep!

Most psychic mediums believe that each of us makes our own future by our past and present actions, and for that reason it is possible to predict the future. That predicted future will not necessarily happen, however, because every individual has free will, can change his mind, and can change events. Although someone's future was leading that person down Road A, with a change of mind, the future may begin to take the person down Road B. Other changes, including the perversity of human nature, may change the situation for the person on Road C.

SIGNS, STORIES, EXPERIMENTS, AND SYMBOLS

During my first marriage, I dreamed I was sitting in the back seat of a car with my friend Stuart. My wife was driving, and Stuart's wife was beside her. The car ran out of control and spun off the road into a terrible crash. I woke up with my heart pounding, just before we were all torn to pieces.

I assumed at the time that the dream represented my emotional problems because Stuart's marriage and mine were showing signs of trouble. The dream came true in that Stuart's marriage ended in failure, as did mine. In my case, we had an actual car accident. The shock of the event brought our problems into the open. The day of the car crash is the day I consider the beginning of the end of my first marriage. So the dream was both a symbol and a prophecy of an actual event. (On a happier note, all parties in the dream now have suitable partners.)

See also: **Disasters, World Events**

AFTERLIFE

Grieving dreams are a powerful argument that dreams have meaning.

DR. PAUL TILLICH, THEOLOGIAN

As a working medium for over 25 years, it comes as no surprise that I receive letters from people who say they've met a dead friend or relative in a dream. In the sleep state, our skeptical, conscious mind takes a back seat for a while, and we are receptive to spontaneous clairvoyance and mediumship.

I have on record many instances telling how the spirit of a loved one appeared in a dream to give verification of the continuation of life after death. Sometimes, the spirit also gives us a little help in sorting out our problems. For example, a woman wrote that she had always been a skeptical person, but that soon after her mother's **death**, her mother appeared in a dream. The mother's spirit looked very concerned and showed a writing desk that the sleeping daughter planned to dispose of. Worried by the dream, the daughter soon visited her mother's house to examine the desk. Slipped under one of the drawers was the mother's will with clear instructions about how the estate should be divided.

In my files, I have numerous examples of dreams in which the dead have helped the living. They have warned of illness, upcoming calamity, and the infidelity of a partner. They have suggested possible changes to prevent unpleasant situations. It is my belief that our dead loved ones do not suddenly gain insight into the future when they pass to the other side, but their ethereal location does give them a better perspective on what is happening around us. Their overview of the situation may enable them to give us wise counsel and guidance to help us make the best decisions about our future. One of the clearest ways to do this is through dreams.

Dreams about the dead are usually vivid and are sometimes set in a place that is a threshold between this world and the next. My files include dreams set at a junction in the road, on a **bridge**, or in front of a **gate** or dark **passage**. In some instances, the dreamer is given a glimpse of the beautiful world that exists beyond life. Reports often include a symbolic barrier of some kind, such as a **door**, **wall**, or **garden fence**. The dreamer is aware that the loved one can go through the gate or obstacle, but the dreamer cannot follow—at least not yet. Nevertheless, the dream meeting may offer a breathtaking glimpse of what waits on the other side. These visions invariably bring comfort and help people to cope with their bereavement.

Based on many reports, contact with spirits in dreams happens either at the time of a death or soon thereafter. Studies by the Society for Psychical Research have shown that a time of emotional crisis is auspicious for a paranormal connection between two empathic people. There are cases where people have seen a phantom of the living person experiencing a dangerous situation. At the point of death, people have often reported that the spirit of the dead or dying person connects with them. For example, I have cases in my files where a person has dreamed of a loved one, awakened during the night, and noticed the **time**. The next morning, the person receives the news that the subject of the dream died at the exact time of the dream. In some instances, the alarm clock has even stopped at the exact time of the death and corresponding dream.

SIGNS, STORIES, EXPERIMENTS, AND SYMBOLS

Of course, not all dreams about spirits are communications from the other side. Remember that dreams may express anxiety and grief about a death. For example, after the death of a partner, the surviving spouse may dream of being **abandoned** or **divorced** by the loved one. Such dreams express the emotional separation of the bereaved dreamer. Similarly, a bereaved person may dream of being **lost** or of missing a train. Again, these dreams express feelings of helplessness and of being out of control after the upheaval.

Most people who have suffered the loss of a loved one will dream of the person during the first six months of bereavement. The loved one will often appear in the dream and then disappear. Although the rational mind knows the loved one has died, the unconscious and the emotions must re-create the loss repeatedly. Dreams help to bring these struggling emotions into balance.

The various stages of bereavement are often accompanied by dreams expressing the emotions associated with the appropriate stage of emotional recovery and adjustment. Here are some of the signs of bereavement and some accompanying dream symbols:

Shock

The shock of a death results in a feeling of disbelief. This acts as a psychological buffer that permits the bereaved to process the reality of loss gradually. Other feelings may include confusion, restlessness, sensations of unreality, **helplessness**, and a state of alarm.

Dreams will reflect these emotional troubles. Dreams may include themes of helplessness, such as being at the mercy of a fierce **monster** or of confusion at being lost in a strange place. Shock may be expressed by sudden occurrences such as **lightning**, loud **explosions**, or accidents. Intertwined with these nightmares may be death and **fear** themes, such as **zombies** or exhuming the body of the dead person. You may dream of being **raped** or **attacked**, expressing feelings of victimization and rejection. In addition, your deceased loved one may appear uncaring or hateful. You may dream of **running** from **shadowy** figures as your emotions attempt to remove you from the painful situation.

Awareness of Loss

As awareness of loss sets in, you may feel separation anxiety and internal conflict, and you may act out emotional expectations or suffer the effects of prolonged stress. Emotions accompanying these states include yearning, crying, and anger or feelings of isolation and betrayal. As a bereaved person, you may displace feelings and blame someone or something else—God or the hospital—for what has happened. You may become angry with yourself, generating feelings of helplessness or guilt. You feel guilty to be alive, for surviving when your loved one did not. If death is seen as a punishment, it may be accompanied by feelings of shame, vulnerability, and fear of death.

Strange dreams may accompany this stage of recovery. Betrayal may appear as a **thief** or **cheat**. Anger may be expressed by

In a dream, the symbolic crossing of a barrier, such as a bridge over a river, can indicate the afterlife.

murder and killing themes, such as hunting, war, and violence. Self-punishment themes in dreams may include hanging, torture, or suicide. Some people dream of punishing the person who has died. Shame and vulnerability may be expressed in themes of nakedness, of being partly dressed or nude in a public place. You may dream of haunted houses, ghosts, and spirits as your unconscious makes you aware of your rejected feelings of fear, uncertainty, and death.

Conservation—Withdrawal

The process of bereavement can be draining, and you may become exhausted from the emotional overload. You may instinctively withdraw from others to conserve energy. You may need to be alone, yet at the same time you may feel isolated and depressed. Although the spiritual hibernation is very difficult, it is usually a time to review what has happened and accept the loss. The grief work at this stage is not easy, and there may still be a lot to let go of regarding the deceased. If you are insistent on retaining the status quo, you may remain at this stage for a long time. Eventually, however, everyone makes the decision to move forward.

Dreams during this stage may express your isolation. The landscapes of the dreams may be bleak. Themes of coldness and ice may appear as representations of the way feelings have become frozen. Dream subjects include locked doors, walking through mud, or cars that won't start. These are all expressions of an inability to move on. Themes indicating depression may be set at night or in gloomy conditions. Occasionally, the deceased may appear in the dream and be unhappy. More often than not, this is a symbolic representation of your own feelings of sorrow as a survivor.

Healing—the Turning Point

Eventually, a turning point comes, and you can begin to move on and make changes in your life. This may include new activities, such as attending college or meeting new people. You are now assuming control and gaining a sense of competence. Your identity is no longer enmeshed with that of the deceased. You may relinquish roles and may give up seeing yourself as a daughter or mother or as a husband or father, for example.

Dreams at this time are likely to include themes of transformation. They may include rebirth themes—snakes shedding their skin or a phoenix or salamander in the fire. Dreams may feature children or babies, representing the new qualities emerging in your own personality. New beginnings are also symbolized by grass during spring or the dawn of the sun. Water themes, suggesting the womb and rebirth, may also feature in dreams of inner transformation. Some dreams may be what Jung called "Grand Dreams" and express philosophical ideas about the purpose of life. These dreams are likely to feature many mythical themes that may describe death, resurrection, and the quest of the hero. During this period, people tend to experience recurring dream themes as the unconscious weaves allegorical stories to express the feelings and inner changes that have been occurring. Periods of transition often bring with them vivid dreams.

Renewal

As a bereaved person, you are not able to enjoy good memories until you face up to the loss. This is a painful process, but it is also a necessary one. Some people get stuck in one or another recovery stages and take years to conclude the bereavement process. Persistent, recurring dreams of death or the themes mentioned above indicate unresolved despair. In such situations, counseling can be beneficial to help the bereaved person progress.

Nothing can ever replace the beloved who is gone, but it is possible to pick up the pieces and move on. After the bereavement is concluded successfully, you may gain new self-awareness and recognize other options in life that can bring happiness. You may now accept responsibility and become self-reliant. Mediumship can help with some stages of the grieving process and reassure the grieving person that life goes on. Making a connection with the spirit through a medium or through mediumistic dreams is much easier once the main grief is resolved. Intense emotions of grief can act as a barrier to communication. Nonetheless, if a connection to spirit is established and verified, it can be very reassuring. Knowing that the loved one is safe and well on the other side may help you let go of the pain and move toward a new way of life. Once the grief is fully healed, it may be possible for you to allow your deceased loved one to draw close in a dream to give you a message of love and hope.

ANIMAL PSYCHICS

Sleep is an acquired habit. Cells don't sleep. Fish swim in the water all night. Even a horse doesn't sleep. A man doesn't need any sleep.

THOMAS EDISON, INVENTOR

Like humans, animals sleep, dream, and may even have psychic dreams. However, nature has devised many different sleep routines, so the experience of sleep and dreams in the animal kingdom may be very different from ours. For example, brown bats sleep 19.9 hours a day, whereas giraffes sleep only 1.9 hours. Amazingly, the brain of a dolphin appears to sleep one hemisphere at a time.

We can't ask them, of course, but animals also appear to dream. They show REM activity and movement during sleep. Watch your dog or cat sleep; you can tell it is dreaming of running. Its eyes twitch, and it may move its paws as if something is happening in the dream. Scientists think that most warm-blooded animals dream and that hunting animals, like cats, dogs, and humans, spend more time dreaming than animals that are hunted, such as cattle, sheep, goats, and rabbits. The opossum is the mammal that dreams the most (and also snores a lot); on the other hand, the spiny anteater, echidna, and platypus never dream. Considering their low intelligence, the platypus and the echidna have huge brains. Scientists speculate that they need this higher brain-to-IQ ratio because they don't have dreams to aid in the learning process.

SIGNS, STORIES, EXPERIMENTS, AND SYMBOLS

It is not known whether animals have psychic dreams or whether they are more psychic than humans. They may have super-sensitive sight, smell, and hearing that make them aware when "their" person is coming home or if something like an earthquake is about to happen. Before the Agadir earthquake in Morocco in 1960, which killed 15,000 people, stray animals, including dogs, were seen streaming from the port. A similar phenomenon was observed three years later in Skopje, Yugoslavia, before the earthquake that reduced that city to rubble.

I have received many stories of psychic animals. These are fascinating examples of animals that know when their owners are coming home, can find their way home over great distances, or know when their owners are ill or upset. Some psychics are able to calm maladjusted pets by using a combination of telepathy and spiritual healing. So, it is reasonable to assume that animals have psychic dreams.

One interesting example was described by English novelist H. Rider Haggard, author of *King Solomon's Mines*. In 1904, Haggard dreamed he saw his daughter's black retriever lying among brushwood by water. The animal, he wrote, "transmitted to my mind in an undefined fashion the knowledge that it was dying." The novelist described the dream to his wife when he awoke.

The next day, the dog was missing, and Haggard and others embarked on a search. The body of the dog was discovered floating against a weir just one mile from his home. Haggard believed that his dream was a telepathic communication with the dying dog, who had communicated with him by "placing whatever portion of my being is capable of receiving such impulses when enchained by sleep, into its own terrible position."

See also: **Animal Symbols, Telepathy**

ANIMAL SPIRITS

Come away, o human child!
To the waters and the wild.

W.B. YEATS, IRISH POET

Many tribal societies believe that the spirits of animals meet people in dreams to give guidance. Shamans claim that they can travel on the astral plane with their "power animals" to distant lands or other dimensions. Tribal cultures recognize a totem animal for the tribe, one for the clan, and one for the family. Similar ideas permeated Celtic cultures, echoes of which may still be found in Ireland.

Sometimes, I sense nature spirits when I walk through the woods or in a place of natural beauty. My hard-to-describe experience is one of being aware of a special atmosphere or energy in the air. I also have a feeling that whatever it is I am sensing, it is conscious but not quite in the same way we would describe animal or human consciousness. Similarly, tribal peoples have spoken about these feelings and personified these forces as fairies, devas, elementals, sprites, and so on. They believe they are guided in their dreams by these powers of nature that appear to them as power animals.

SIGNS, STORIES, EXPERIMENTS, AND SYMBOLS

According to shamans, a totem/power animal that comes to you in a dream represents qualities you need but that are hidden or obscured. Some of the most common power animals include:

Bear: Bears hibernate in the winter and are, therefore, associated with dreams, prophecy, and introspection. A bear cave can symbolize

Animal spirits can act as powerful allies in the world of dreams.

the womb of Mother Earth. Native Americans believe that people with Bear Medicine are self-sufficient and independent.

Buffalo: Many Native American tribes consider the buffalo the symbol of abundance because it was a primary source of meat and clothing for the tribe. Buffalo Medicine symbolizes a reverence for Mother Nature.

Cat: Sacred to the ancient Egyptians, cats are associated with mystery and clairvoyance. As a power animal, a cat may represent your intuitive abilities or magical powers. In Scandinavia, cats are considered fertility symbols.

Deer: These animals denote people who are swift and alert. Their perceptions are very keen and may include the psychic sixth sense. Gentleness and grace are also traditional characteristics associated with these totem animals.

Dog: A person with a dog power animal is said to be devoted to family and friends.

Dolphin: Dolphins represent kindness and playfulness. Dolphin Medicine includes change, wisdom, balance, harmony, communication skills, and freedom.

Eagle: The eagle is a symbol of power, healing, and wisdom associated with the Great Spirit. It may also represent the power of clear vision.

Horse: A horse power animal brings stamina and mobility. A horse also represents loyalty, devotion, and faithfulness. Horses are also associated with travel.

Lion: The lion denotes power. As a teacher, it shows the importance of remaining confident.

Owl: The owl's powers include discrimination and truth. It has keen sight and is silent and swift. The owl is the messenger of secrets and omens.

Rabbit: The timid rabbit represents wit in the face of fear. As a power animal, it brings modesty and quick thinking.

Wolf: Native Americans regard wolves as teachers and pathfinders. As a power animal, a wolf brings self-confidence and the courage to face change.

ANIMAL SYMBOLS

Horse sense is the thing a horse has which keeps it from betting on itself.

W. C. FIELDS, ACTOR

Animals often appear in dreams as symbols that represent aspects of ourselves, in particular, our instinctive nature. A **monkey** may symbolize a mischievous nature, a **cow** may show docility, a rat may represent sneakiness, and a tiger may portray anger. Similarly, a dog may represent devotion; a cat, intuition; and a pig, gluttony. We use many animal symbols in everyday language, calling people sly as a **fox**, slippery as a fish, strong as an **ox**, or cunning as a snake. In most instances, creatures that appear in dreams may be understood as projections of human qualities, and you need remember this when making your dream interpretations.

Dreams about animals and birds may also represent messages coming from the unconscious. Frightening animals may represent issues you refuse to face in waking life that the unconscious is encouraging you to address. Birds may show an opportunity to transcend problems and gain spiritual freedom. They may show the feelings you have about a relationship. A thieving bird like a **magpie** may represent adultery, and a territorial bird like a **blackbird** may show jealousy. So, first look for the symbolic meaning of dream animals to reveal what they are saying about you and your feelings.

Of interest is a dream Napoleon Bonaparte had. Napoleon ignored a prophetic dream that occurred the night before his defeat at Waterloo. The dream depicted two cats scurrying between two armies; his cat was killed. If he had heeded the dream and prevented the battle, Europe might have a different political landscape today.

Tradition has it that creatures in dreams are augurs of the future. After traveling extensively and interviewing people about the outcome of their dreams, Artemidorus, a Greek living in 200 A.D., wrote a book about how to interpret dreams. Centuries later, when Gutenberg finished printing the first Bible, the next book to be published was the *Oneirocritica of Artemidorus*.

SIGNS, STORIES, EXPERIMENTS, AND SYMBOLS

Some of the traditional meanings for animals and other creatures appearing in dreams have been greatly influenced by the *Oneirocritica of Artemidorus*. Here are a few examples:

Alligator, crocodile: Be aware that enemies are plotting against you. Someone may "snap" a lot.

Animals: If animals are calm, business will succeed; if they are hostile, expect failure.

Ants: Good fortune is coming. If they infest a house, hard work is ahead.

Ape: Caution! Someone is up to mischief.

Bees: Good news and financial success are on their way, but if a beehive is empty, so too will be your bank account. Killing bees means ruin, but dreaming of beeswax foretells a love affair.

Beetles: You have enemies who may harm you. Killing beetles means temporary difficulties.

Birds: Birds are generally a sign of good luck unless they are dead, which foretells dark times. The Egyptians believed that catching a bird augured the loss of something precious. The Assyrians believed that meeting a bird signified the return of lost property.

Butterfly: You will achieve social success. Buy yourself a new outfit!

Cat: This is a prediction of treachery and deceit. Napoleon is reported to have had a dream of a black cat the night before the battle of Waterloo.

Cattle: Peace and prosperity are on the way.

Cuckoo: You will learn upsetting news.

Dog: This is good fortune if the dog is large and friendly. The opposite is true if the dog is angry.

Dragon: Someone in authority will help you.

Eagle: For the ancient Greeks, this symbolized a leader.

Elephant: In the East and West, an elephant brings great good luck. Hannibal attributed the battle plan to attack Rome over the Alps with elephants to something that came to him in a dream.

Fish: Catching a fish means you will be prosperous. Dead fish mean disappointments.

Flies: Little things will irritate you.

Goat: Bad luck for gamblers and thieves, particularly if they stole this book!

Horse: This augurs good luck, unless you dream of falling off. A horse being shod means you will receive money.

Insects: Many small problems are afoot.

Jackdaw: This denotes illness and arguments; if you kill a jackdaw, you will own a property.

Kangaroo: You will outwit a sneaky enemy. You're one jump ahead.

Lion: A lion predicts a rise to social and financial prominence.

Lizard: A friend is not true. Someone may attack you.

Lobster: You will be showered with riches, but beware of hedonism.

Mice: Your friends and loved ones are insincere.

Newt: A Turk will hit you in the face with an empty hot water bottle. (I made that one up, so you won't take these too seriously.)

Owl: This bird indicates setbacks and disappointments. The Romans believed owls brought bad luck.

Parrot: You are wasting your time and chattering too much.

Pigeons: To the ancient Greeks, wild pigeons were a dream symbol for immoral women.

Pigs: All will go well at work, but there may be domestic troubles. If a fisherman dreams of pigs, superstition says he'll have a bad catch.

Quail: A favorable omen if they're alive, but dead quail indicate illness.

Rabbits: Rabbits foretell changes for the better and potential prosperity. White rabbits indicate fidelity.

Rats: Misfortune and clandestine plots are working against you.

Snakes: Generally, these mean bad luck and evil forces at work, but the Egyptians believed snakes were a good omen, showing that the dreamer would soon settle a dispute. Similarly, the Assyrians believed if a snake is seized in a dream, you will have the protection of angels. For the Hebrews, a snake bite meant a doubled income.

Spider: You will be energetic and very lucky. If a spider bites you, your partner is unfaithful.

Tiger: If a tiger comes toward you, your enemies will take advantage of you. If it is caged, you will be the victor.

Toad: Your reputation will be in tatters because of a scandal.

Vulture: Someone is scheming against you. A woman will be harmed by gossip and slander.

Worms: A worm denotes illness if it is alive but good fortune if it is dead or used as bait.

Zebra: Many changes lie ahead, and you will be engaged in fleeting enterprises.

BANAL PSYCHIC DREAMS

*You know it's Monday when you wake
up and it feels like Tuesday.*

JIM DAVIS, CARTOONIST

My father told me his dream about sailing up the Amazon River. In the dream, he was with two women, both of whom drowned. The next day, he opened his newspaper to read that reports had come overnight about two women explorers who had drowned while making an expedition up the Amazon River. There was no way he could have seen this information in advance.

What intrigued me about his description was that the dream was so matter-of-fact and yet had no bearing on his life whatsoever. It is curious that some of the most accurate psychic dreams come to people who have no interest in what is being shown. There is no emotional content to the dreams and nothing that relates to the dreamer's own life. The dreamer is not able to influence the events that have been revealed. The dream has no special significance to the dreamer.

So, why do we get these seemingly meaningless clairvoyant glimpses? Could it be that some psychic dreams are simply stray signals that we accidentally connect to—like a crossed telephone connection? Some psychologists argue that human consciousness extends to the quantum level where it is possible for past and present to happen simultaneously and for an object to exist in two places at once.

Memory itself may not be dependent on the chemistry of the brain but somehow be wired into this quantum level of existence. This may explain why memory is retained during a near-death experience or how a person may lie on an operating table and be able to "step outside his body" and observe himself from the ceiling. And since everything is connected at a subatomic level, perhaps all consciousness is interconnected through what mystics call the universal mind.

In sleep, we connect to the universal mind and, therefore, sometimes observe seemingly banal events that have no significance to us whatsoever and that are completely removed from our own experience. At best, these weird "coincidences" may make us question the relationship between mind and matter and between inner and outer experience and help us form a broader view of the nature of reality.

SIGNS, STORIES, EXPERIMENTS, AND SYMBOLS

When we dream, the most bizarre events are treated with nonchalance, and it is easy to miss important information being given about the future. For example, when I was in the advertising business, I dreamed about a building with a row of fountains leading to it. In the dream, I met an old customer who talked to me about how his business had changed. Soon afterward, I received a call from an old customer (not the man in the dream) who asked if I would visit his new offices to bid on a new project. I did not know that the company had vastly grown in size.

As I approached the new offices, I was astonished to see the row of fountains flanking either side of the driveway and frantically tried to recall the detailed advice I had been given. This dream didn't appear to be important on awakening, but it proved to be significant later when I examined my dream diary. The most apparently trivial dreams can prove to be the most interesting.

See also: **Serialism, Universal Mind**

BIBLICAL PROPHECIES

*If there is a prophet among you, I the Lord
make myself known to him in a vision,
I speak with him in a dream.*

NUMBERS 12:6

The Bible contains over 50 references to dreams. One of the earliest and most well-known is Jacob's dream of a ladder from Earth to Heaven. In the dream, God promised Jacob that all the families on earth would be blessed through Abraham, Isaac, and Jacob. God would return Jacob to the Promised Land.

Dreams caused great trouble for Joseph and his brothers. "Here comes the dreamer," say the brothers. "Let us slay him, and then let us see what will become of his dreams" (Genesis 32:19). Joseph is thrown into a pit and eventually sold to traders, who bring him to Egypt. But Joseph's understanding of prophetic dreams also brought him good fortune as well. His interpretation of the Pharaoh's dreams led to his appointment as viceroy of Egypt and saved his family from famine.

It was a dream that foretold to Abraham his people's slavery in Egypt and the eventual Exodus. "A deep slumber descended upon Abraham and a horror of a great darkness enveloped him....Your seed will be a stranger in a land that is not theirs, and will serve them, and they will afflict them...."(Genesis 15:12-13). The covenant between God, Abraham, and the people of Israel was revealed in association with this dream. Similarly, Muhammad received much of the text of the Koran in a dream, and he often interpreted his disciples' dreams.

As described in the book of Daniel, the dream of Nebuchadnezzar, king of Babylon, is also an important biblical dream. Nebuchadnezzar dreamed of a tree being felled and of being left to graze like a beast. Daniel explained that this dream was to teach him to acknowledge the heavenly power above him in the same way as he was above the beasts in the field. The dream was thought to be prophetic.

Nebuchadnezzar eventually went insane, and his son Balshazzar assumed the throne. During a feast given by Balshazzar, Daniel saw a message of judgment in God's handwriting on the palace wall. He interpreted the writing to the king, "Thou art weighed in the balances, and art found wanting. Thy kingdom is divided, and given to the Medes and Persians" (Daniel 5:25-30). That very night, the Medo-Persian army captured Babylon and killed Balshazzar, and King Darius became ruler.

Many Christians taught that God might reveal himself through dreams. St. John Chrysostom said that we are not responsible for our dreams and should not be ashamed of what we dream or of any images that appear in them. Dreams changed the lives of St. Augustine and St. Jerome. In time, dreams fell out of fashion within Christianity. Martin Luther, the founder of Protestantism, believed that dreams were the work of the devil. Luther said that sin was "the confederate and father of foul dreams." Since the church interpreted God's word, revelations made to individuals in dreams could only come from the devil.

SIGNS, STORIES, EXPERIMENTS, AND SYMBOLS

Psychologist Carl Jung made some interesting observations about religion and dreams. He believed that religious experiences were found in the human psyche and not in the supernatural. He took an interest in Gnosticism and claimed that the Gnostics were akin to psychologists. One Gnostic idea that Jung explained in his psychology was that Christ was the symbolic representation of the self and could be compared to other mythic gods who die young and are born again. Jung caused turmoil within Christianity by claiming that the **Trinity** was a symbol for psychological processes. The Father symbolized the psyche in its original, undifferentiated wholeness; the Son represented the human psyche; and the Holy Spirit was the state of self-critical submission to a higher reality.

Religious symbols may appear in a dream when you are undergoing some form of spiritual inner transformation. **Religious figures** may represent your higher self, guiding you to self-realization. Similarly, **holy buildings** may symbolize the spiritual aspects of your nature.

In the past, people used bibliomancy to interpret a dream's prophecy. On awakening, the dreamer opened the Bible at random, closed his eyes, and pointed to a line of text. This was then interpreted. Religious symbols also appear in dream prophecies of the superstitious. Writers of superstition dream books were probably persecuted for their beliefs because most religious dreams are bad omens. Here are a few amusing examples:

Abbey: If it is in ruins, then so will be your plans. For a woman, it may foretell an illness.

Abbess: If she is smiling, true friends will surround you. But for a woman to dream of an abbess shows that she will be "compelled to perform distasteful tasks." The mind boggles!

Abbot: Plots will lead to your downfall.

Adam and Eve: You will be robbed of your success.

Altar: Quarrels lie ahead.

Baptism: You must practice temperance.

Bible: Disillusionment will occur as a result of sensual enjoyment.

Bishop: This is a bad dream for authors and teachers, who will be hampered by worries.

Blasphemy: A friend is really an enemy.

Chalice: You will prosper at another's expense.

Christ: You will find peace, wealth, and knowledge.

Church: Disappointments in pleasure lie ahead. Sometimes, this denotes a funeral.

Cross: Trouble lies ahead. If someone carries the cross, you will be asked to help missionaries. Get yourself a mosquito net.

Holy Communion: You will give in to frivolous desires. This is not a good dream for shopaholics.

Hymns: These indicate harmony at home and a steady business.

Monk: A monk foretells family arguments and unpleasant journeys.

Nun: For a man, it means material joys, but for a woman this dream bodes discontentment.

Pilgrims: You will go on a journey.

Quaker: You have faithful friends; for a woman, the dream shows she will have a happy marriage.

Satan: Dangerous adventures are ahead. They require careful strategy.

Steeple: This warns of sickness and difficulties.

Vatican: You will receive unexpected favors.

Vicar: Your bad temper will cause you to do foolish things.

See also: **Future**, **Prophecy**, **Tribal Dream Interpretation**

BIRTH

Struggling in my father's hands,
Striving against my swaddling bands,
Bound and weary, I thought best
To sulk upon my mother's breast.

WILLIAM BLAKE, BRITISH POET

The dreams of pregnant women are often very vivid and may tell the expectant mother things about the baby she is carrying. Legends say that the Buddha appeared before birth in a dream to his mother in the form of an elephant. Similarly, an angel foretold the birth of Jesus to Mary. There is a centuries-long tradition in the Orient in which women are specially blessed with prophetic dreams that foretell the conception, sex, personality, and fate of their future children. In modern Korea, most expectant mothers claim to have these mysterious dreams. They are usually kept secret from the child but remain an inspiration to the parents to guide the child's path through life.

One function of dreams is to help overcome emotional problems and traumas that occur in waking life. Sometimes, they bring to the surface issues that have been pushed into the background of our awareness, such as fears and worries we refuse to face. In particular, nightmares force dreamers to take notice of things they refuse to face up to, including current emotional problems and ones going back to early childhood and infancy.

One of life's most traumatic experiences is the experience of birth. Whether you were born naturally, with the help of forceps, or by Caesarean section, you left a warm and nurturing environment for the bright lights of the real world. Birth is a momentous occasion that happens to every one of us. Some therapists claim that the trauma is so great that we block the memory to protect ourselves psychologically.

Dreams may try to recall the repressed memories of birth. I have a recurring dream that I believe to be a dream about my own birth. It involves sensations of confinement, frustration, and helplessness and includes feelings that are very hard to describe. Although the dream is upsetting, it is also fascinating. When it occurs, I allow myself to return to it, whenever possible. In this way, I believe, I have gradually accepted the traumatic events at the start of my life and can now continue without repressed fears of birth in the background of my consciousness.

Dreams help bring about spiritual wholeness. Integrating the memories of birth is one segment of finding completeness. Once the fear of birth is overcome, I believe the door is open to allowing other early memories to come into consciousness. These include pre-birth memories of the heavenly worlds and previous incarnations.

Some therapists claim the trauma of birth colors the way you perceive yourself and influences all of your actions in life. If you could recall the events and see them from the standpoint of an observer—rather than as you felt them at the time—your perception of life would be altered.

Rebirthers go back and re-experience their transition into the world by means of hypnosis. During the hypnosis session, they will often writhe about, moving their shoulders from side to side in an effort to push through the birth canal. Some report squeezing sensations around the head followed by blinding lights. Some even speak about being held upside down or spanked on the backside.

Whether these retrieved memories are real or not cannot be tested, but the emotional experience of this "recall" is claimed to be of benefit. It is said to be emotionally uplifting, giving the subject a completely new perspective on life. It may lift depression and increase the subject's confidence and sense of self-worth. The rebirther is now prepared to embrace life with the new-found optimism that comes from negating the fears that arose at the start of life.

A full rebirthing session is best done under the supervision of a therapist. This person may introduce special body movements and specific voice commands. The therapist may play recordings of a baby's heartbeat to induce a semi-hypnotic state to connect subjects to their birth memories. Dreams can take people to this point in life spontaneously and without rebirthing therapy. If this should occur, accept the experience as valuable. Instead of rejecting it as a nightmare, consider going with the dream and discovering the possibilities that birth recall has to offer.

BUILDINGS AND PLACES

There is but one temple in the Universe, and that is the body of man.

NOVALIS, GERMAN POET

I had a puzzling dream that I wrote up in my dream diary. I was learning to fly an airplane with a group of uneducated Arabs at a flying school in Florida. The dream seemed fairly unimportant but took on a special significance a few days later. September 11, 2001, is etched in people's memories as the day terrorists destroyed the World Trade Center and damaged the Pentagon. It turned out later that the terrorist hijackers got pilot training at private aviation centers in Florida.

What puzzles me most about the dream is that it was so uninteresting. You would think a dream of these upcoming momentous events would have been a little more exciting! At first, I assumed the dream had something to do with memories of my days running an advertising agency because one of my London-based clients had some years before bought a flying school in Kissimmee, Florida. In retrospect, the dream may have used my existing memories to show me associated events. The closest association I had was my knowledge of the Kissimmee Flying School.

Psychic dreams often foreshadow dramatic world events. Another dream that interested me was sent to one of my columns in a Scottish newspaper by a worried woman who wrote, "I kept having terrible repetitive

Buildings and places often represent the dreamer.
Sometimes they represent actual locations that will prove important.

nightmares of a nuclear disaster by a tall tower. I would thrash in my sleep and was heard to call out 'The Russians! The Russians!' The meaning of my nightmares was revealed on the television some weeks later. I saw on the news a picture of the very tower I had just been dreaming about: the Chernobyl power station in Russia." Interestingly, the famous seventeeth-century Scottish psychic dreamer Kenneth Mackenzie (also known as the Brahan Seer) predicted the fallout from Chernobyl, saying, "Deer and other wild animals shall be exterminated by horrid black rain."

Clearly, some dreams about buildings may contain insight into events that will take place. In dreams, buildings and places are mainly symbols for the human body or our psychological state of mind. For example, the upstairs of a building may represent your conscious mind, and the lower floors or cellar, your hidden self. A discovery about yourself (or even a clairvoyant glimpse of the future) may be symbolized by what you discover in a **basement** or **cellar**. A building such as a **church** or **abbey** may represent the mansion of the soul, the whole person. A **bedroom** may symbolize secrets, rest, or sexual matters. A **factory** or **office** may highlight work issues, and a **farm** may point to animal instincts or suggest a need to simplify life. **Government buildings** may represent morality; and **libraries**, knowledge. The condition of the buildings may express the way you feel about yourself or may highlight health issues. A decayed building may be the harbinger of an illness.

In addition to the psychological meaning of buildings, many traditional meanings are taken as augurs of the future.

The table on the following page shows some of the traditional dream meanings associated with buildings and places. Some superstitions need to be taken with a grain of salt. See the **Symbolism** entry for advice about the psychological way to interpret dream meanings.

CLAIRVOYANCE

Intuition comes very close to clairvoyance; it appears to be the extra sensory perception of reality.

ALEXIS CARREL, FRENCH SURGEON

Strictly speaking, clairvoyance is the para-normal ability to obtain information about an object or event without the use of the known senses. However, as it is generally used, clairvoyance refers to many psychic gifts such as telepathy, mediumship, second sight, prophetic vision, and psychic dreams. Clairvoyance literally means "clear seeing," and is often used to refer to visionary psychic experiences. For example, a medium will describe the pictures he sees given to him by a spirit as clairvoyance. The words he may "hear" from spirit, such as names, come from clairaudience ("clear hearing"), and the sensations, such as bodily ailments at the time of the spirit's death, are described as clairsentience ("clear sensing").

An example of dream clairvoyance would be dreaming about something that is not known by anyone else so that it could not be received from another person's mind by telepathy. Visiting a location in a dream and spotting something unusual that later proves to be true is an example of clairvoyance.

Good Omen		Bad Omen	
Abbey	This only means good luck if you see it in daylight.	Attic	Bad omen or good omen? This means casual promiscuity.
Castle	If in good repair, this brings good fortune, but bad temper is shown if it is in ruins.	Bricks	Unfavorable changes lie ahead.
Cemetery	This is good fortune, of course.	Church	An ill omen if you are inside.
Circus	Improvements in your finances lie ahead.	Fortress	To be imprisoned in a fortress shows that your enemies will win.
Factory	Reward comes after a struggle.	Gold mine	Do not speculate or there will be loss.
Forest	You will overcome worry.	Holiday (or Vacation)	Great hard work is coming.
Gallows	Good luck will come to you.	House (small)	Money trouble lies ahead.
Garage	This foretells fortunate improvements.	Homebuying	This foretells a troublesome love affair.
Greenhouse	Love will grow.	Hills	There will be many difficulties to overcome.
Harem	You will have a busy social life (if you ever decide to go out).	Iceberg	You will have secret opposition.
Hotel	You can expect luck in love.	Inn	Poverty and failure lie in the future. A family member may go to prison.
House	You'll have security and wealth if the house is big.	Jail	Hard times lie ahead.
House (selling)	You'll experience a release from responsibilities.	Quarry	This is an omen of a death or disaster.
Island	New opportunities and developments are waiting.	Quicksand	This foretells health problems.
Office	Personal relationships are soon to change.	Racecourse	You are in danger of losing money because of fraud.
Park	A happy love affair is in your future.	Restaurant	If the meal is expensive, expect setbacks in your social life.
Party	A happy social life is yours.	School	There will be difficulties if you are at school, but you'll have success if you pass by one.
Pyramid	This indicates success through travel.	Tunnel	Any changes you make may be risky.
Zoo	Unexpected and enjoyable travel lie ahead.	Volcano	Beware of dishonest people.

Clairvoyance is closely linked to "remote viewing" and was used during the Cold War to spy on Soviet military bases. In some instances, psychics working with the CIA were asked to spy on Soviet military bases in their dreams. They had many remarkable successes and were able to provide verifiable information about the chosen targets.

SIGNS, STORIES, EXPERIMENTS, AND SYMBOLS

Remote viewing is a comparatively easy clairvoyant skill to learn, and you may currently be showing signs of having this ability. Your dreams may already spontaneously reveal clairvoyant knowledge about distant locations.

Remote viewing skills can be improved through practice. You can set up experiments with your friends. You can take turns setting up an object at a specific location. Write down your dreams every night to see if the target object is featured in the dream. Compare notes once a week. You may find that your subconscious may distort the image. If, for example, your friend chose a child's toy, you may that night have dreamed of children, or if it was a box of cereal, you may have dreamed of eating. Keep trying the experiments, and the pictures that come to you will become more specific.

See also: **Extra Sensory Perception (ESP), Remote Viewing (RV)**

COINCIDENCE AND SYNCHRONICITY

Next week is another day.

PEADAR CLOHESSY, IRISH POLITICIAN

Psychologist Carl Jung believed that a person's inner state could somehow affect the physical world and explain why meaningful coincidences happened when a person was undergoing therapy or spiritual change. Jung developed a theory he called "synchronicity," in which he attempted to explain events that were meaningfully but not causally connected.

Jung claimed that coincidences didn't just happen but were the result of inner processes. Because of this, dreams may sometimes find expression through odd events that happen in waking life. And just as dreams reflect events in life, so too, life events may be reflections of dreams.

My spiritual work brings me in contact with many people who are undergoing profound spiritual change. The people may be bereaved, may have suffered a life-changing calamity, or may be seeking to develop their own spiritual and psychic powers. Often, they speak about how circumstances have occurred that appear to lead them to me or to other spiritual teachers. It is as if you have an inner knowing that guides your feet for a while and ensures that you encounter the people you need to meet at that time. Some people discover this when they meet their life partner. The liaison is often more than coincidence; there is a feeling of events conspiring for you to be together. In the same way, you appear to be led to meet important friends or experience things that are to change your life.

If you experience a strange synchronicity in relation to a dream, it raises some interesting questions. Perhaps strange coincidences occur when your spiritual progress requires that your path be nudged subconsciously toward the right place or person for assistance. There is a sense of connectivity to something greater than yourself, and you may have a feeling of being drawn toward self-realization. Similarly, anti-synchronicity may help you avoid paths that would be detrimental to your well-being, such as canceling a journey because of a hunch and discovering later that an accident occurred.

Could it be that inner forces sometimes determine external events? Subjective experience may prove this is the case. I believe the inner world determines what you encounter in life, and I hold to the maxim that "as you think, so things become." In part, events are determined by "karma," the accumulated merit or fault gathered from actions, but I believe inner conditions have the greatest influence on personal destiny.

Perhaps nothing at all is random, and all the good and bad fortune you encounter are just the unfolding of karma and thought. People blame luck for their troubles, but if what I have explained holds true, you initiate everything that happens to you. You choose your lot and can be your own executioner, or you can use your free will to bring about a fortunate life. This is the purpose of psychic dreams: to guide you in making the best choices and to prompt you toward a path that encourages the cultivation of the inner life. Psychic dreams are most likely to occur at times of momentous inner change as part of the process of spiritual integration.

SIGNS, STORIES, EXPERIMENTS, AND SYMBOLS

At a critical point in a consultation, a beetle flew into Jung's office as his patient described a dream about a **scarab**. The scarab is an Egyptian symbol of rebirth, and Jung noted that the auspicious moment of the flying **beetle** entering the room coincided with the patient's need to be freed from her excessive rationalism. It was as if events had conspired to help trigger the necessary inner process by challenging the patient's rationality.

If you learn to link to your subconscious psychic streams, Fate may give you a helping hand and guide you toward self-knowledge. The startling opportunities that synchronicity provides can be amazing.

See also: **Future**, **Time**

CRYSTALS

Nature has never made two human beings, two planets, or two crystals alike. Consider the magnitude of that diversity.

BARBARA WALKER, AUTHOR

New Age crystal healers attribute great power to certain rocks, minerals, precious metals, semi-precious stones, and crystals to help provide restful sleep. These healers also point to connections between crystals and dreaming. They say that crystals placed underneath the pillow can aid in healing.

Many crystal healers believe that clear quartz is an important tool in communication with the spirit world. It can channel communication in dreams when placed under the head during sleep because it induces a very deep and restful sleep. Similarly, rutilated quartz is believed to energize the mind during REM and induce psychic dreams. Smoky quartz is believed to empower people to reach goals set during psychic dreams. It is also believed to increase dream lucidity and help guide spirits in mediumistic dreams.

Some other crystal aids to psychic dreaming include:

Astral Travel: The tiny, double-terminated quartz crystals of Herkimer diamonds may induce astral projection and dream journeys.

Dream Recall: Beta quartz or star garnet may help induce dream recall. Similarly, amber, although not a crystal, is believed to help memory and can be used to help sleep learning. This may be useful after reviewing before an exam.

Dream Interpretation: Diaspor is believed to help unravel the meaning of dreams, as are green sapphire, kyanite, red jasper, and lapis.

Nightmares: Opal and ruby are believed to induce happy dreams and dispel nightmares.

DEATH AND DYING

Death is one of the few things that can be done as easily lying down. The difference between sex and death is that with death you can do it alone and no one is going to make fun of you.

WOODY ALLEN, FILMMAKER

Dreams about **death** and dying may be upsetting, but they are not necessarily dark prophecies of the future. These dreams are so common that if they all came true there would hardly be anyone left alive. The truth is that nearly all dreams of death and dying are metaphors that express feelings.

Death may represent the end of one phase so that a new one may begin. This symbol of finality may also represent a major change in your life, such as the end of a relationship or career. Similarly, a dream about death can symbolize important changes in your behavior. For example, you may decide to stop behaving in a childish way and then dream about a child dying. You may fear that you are neglecting the parental side of your nature and subsequently dream about your mother or father dying. The dream may be telling you to be more maternal and caring. If you dream of a death, you should ask yourself, "Which aspect of myself does this person represent?" If you answer honestly, you will probably see that the dream is about you and your feelings rather than a prophecy for the future.

If a situation in life is becoming too much to handle, you may dream of being a **corpse**. The dream may be saying, "This will be the death of me," or "This situation is killing me." When you say these kinds of things in everyday conversation, you don't mean people to take you literally. So, too, dreams express your feelings in a figurative way. A cold corpse may represent the coldness of your feelings and may be a call for you to be more compassionate. Similarly, a **burial**, **coffin**, or **funeral** might symbolize the emotions and feelings that you try to push out of your conscious thoughts and bury in your subconscious. You may feel that part of yourself or something in your life has died. You may be grieving for something that has disappeared from your life, such as a loving relationship or a situation in which you were happy and secure. Of course, these dreams may also be about your feelings of bereavement connected to a death that occurred in the past. The dream may be saying, "I feel just as upset now as when so and so died."

Sigmund Freud had a lot to say about dreams about death. He believed that everyone has two contending basic drives:

eros, the drive toward pleasure and life, and *thanatos*, the drive toward death. The "death instinct" identified by Freud is the desire to give up the struggles of life and return to quiescence and the grave. Death symbolism in dreams may indicate that you have feelings of despair and need to address these negative tendencies.

Clearly, if you have a dream about death, you should first consider whether the dream is about you and your feelings or about events that are to take place. However, in some rare instances, dreams about death may predict future events. For example, my grandmother had such a dream on the night before my sister's wedding. When she awoke from the upsetting dream, she told my aunt about it. She dreamed that my sister was wearing a black wedding dress and that the groom was nowhere to be found. Six months after the wedding, my sister's husband was diagnosed with cancer. Six months after that, he died. Obviously, my grandmother's dream of the bride wearing black was a symbol of the tragedy that was to come.

Examining dreams I have had that have foretold of a death and similar dreams sent to me, I have noticed that there are some qualities of precognitive dreams that are very different from the death dreams I described at the start of this entry. One major difference is that dreams that predict a death are usually without fear and emotion. They are very vivid, but they are matter-of-fact. Dreams about death that are filled with upsetting feelings are usually expressions of your emotions. Dreams about actual death are usually stated as a fait accompli and are generally not accompanied by upsetting feelings. Often they are filled with symbols of hope and the promise of the continuation of life beyond death.

I believe that it is possible to "feel" whether the figure of the dead in a dream is only a symbol or should be taken literally. Once you enter middle age, it is more likely that you will begin to have death dreams. As you continue to age and death becomes even more of an issue, the likelihood of death dreams increases.

Psychologists have made some interesting studies of the dreams of patients who thought they were going to die or who died suddenly. In most instances, these dreams imply not an end to earthly existence but a transformation and a continuation of life. Carl Jung emphasized that the unconscious psyche pays little attention to the sudden end of bodily life and behaves as if the life of the individual will continue. The unconscious "believes" in a life after death.

Dreams contain many symbols of death and subsequent rebirth into a new and transformed state of being. However, you need to remember that some of the symbols appearing in death dreams are images that are also present during what Jung called the "individuation process," the growth into psychological wholeness. These images are especially likely to appear in dreams during the second half of life.

SIGNS, STORIES, EXPERIMENTS, AND SYMBOLS

Angels: As well as being messengers from God, mythology has it that angels are the beings that take a dying person away from life to a better world. Jungian psychology may liken the angel to the **anima**, the perfect woman that in reality is symbolic of the female aspect of the man's psyche. She may appear in dreams as a guiding figure. (A woman has an **animus** figure, the psychological symbol for the perfect man and male aspect of her own nature.) These figures often appear in dreams as a person strives toward psychological wholeness. People who are terminally ill may dream of their anima/animus figure as a guide to the next life. This was the case with the Greek philosopher Socrates, who dreamed of a radiant white woman while he was in prison. He took this to be an announcement of his death. My own work as a medium has led me to meet dying people, who at the time of their death, have seen a being of light standing in the room. Their joyful descriptions of the "vision" they have convinces me that their experience is much more than a psychological process.

Animals: Death may be symbolized by a **dog** or a **wolf**. When Jung's mother died, he dreamed of a giant wolfhound, crashing in the undergrowth. He wrote, "It tore past me, and I suddenly knew: the Wild Huntsman had commanded it to carry away a human soul… The next morning I received the news of my mother's passing." Similarly, a dead animal or bird may represent a human death. A **dove** may symbolize the flight of the soul after death. In ancient Egypt, the Ka (soul) was represented by a bird or winged figure.

Bridge: Crossing a bridge may represent the transition to the next life. In the Islamic tradition, the deceased must cross over the perilously thin Sirat Bridge to get to the afterlife. In the same fashion, the entryway to the next world may appear as a dark passage, similar in some ways to the birth canal that brought us into life in the first place. Many ancient cultures used to bury their dead in the embryonic position as a symbol of rebirth in a new life.

Burglar: The closeness of death is sometimes represented in dreams by a burglar. Like death, this person is someone unfamiliar and enters one's present life unexpectedly.

Fire: A flame may represent the life force and spirit. To dream of a flame being put out can represent a death. In the past, people would light candles in a mortuary room as an allegory for giving new life and consciousness to the deceased. To this day, we still light candles in churches as a symbol of life and remembrance. Fire is also a symbol for transformation. This may indicate the transformation of the person as they move from this world to the next, or more likely, it will show psychological transformations that are happening within the dreamer.

Flowers: Flowers are a typical symbol for postmortal existence or for the resurrection of a person after death. Wreaths of flowers at a funeral symbolize not only our feelings of sympathy but also our hidden desire for the departed to find a new life. In a dream, flowers may also show our search for wholeness. Flowers are generally shaped like a mandala, which makes them a fitting symbol for the self. A **lotus** may show enlightenment and triumph over death.

Journeys: Death may be symbolized as a great passage or a journey. This may include crossing over water as in the Orphic and Elysian mysteries of the journey with the boatman Charon to the glorious Elysium or the "Isles of the Blessed." Sometimes, the journey is to the **West**, the place of the setting sun.

Trees: A tree often symbolizes the life of an individual. A tree is also like the human nervous system. Cutting down the tree of life in a dream may represent the ending of a life.

For some critically ill patients, a tree that is cut down represents brutal surgical intervention. Alternatively, this image may represent your own feelings of despair and may show a need to embrace life rather than deny it. (The ancient Assyrians claimed that to dream of cutting down a date palm signified a solution to the dreamer's problems.)

Vegetation: A field that has been cut down or a mown lawn may represent the end of life. The grim reaper carries a scythe. In ancient mythology, wheat and barley are important symbols of the rebirth that follows bodily death. In Egyptian tombs, images are sometimes shown of the dead body of Osiris sprouting new, healthy body parts to replace damaged, diseased ones. Seeds were often put in a mummy's bandages. The image of a **green man** can represent both death and rebirth. In a dream, these symbols may show the continuation of the life process after death. They may also be symbols for personal transformation.

Water: Water can represent the life force. It may also represent the waters of the womb and the possibility of rebirth. Often the ashes of the dead are cast onto a river or the ocean.

Wedding: According to Jungian psychology, a wedding is the union of psychic opposites: the high and low, the conscious and unconscious, and, in particular, the male and female aspects of the personality. Jung wrote of the *hierosgamos*, sacred marriage, as a symbol for the "death wedding." A wedding is a symbol of a turning point in life and perhaps also a symbol of completeness. When Jung came close to death, he dreamed of a mystical marriage in a garden of pomegranates. The dream included ecstatic visions that made Jung's waking life appear gray in comparison. Of course, weddings can also symbolize other things, too, such as a coming together of opposites within the personality or a real-life relationship.

See also: **Afterlife**

DISASTERS

The future will be better tomorrow.

AL GORE, FORMER VICE PRESIDENT OF THE UNITED STATES

Dreams about the future are often filled with themes of "doom and gloom" and may include predictions of catastrophe, calamity, and disaster. In the "**Accidents**" section, I explain how these may sometimes be symbols of our own emotional state, but there are instances when dreams speak about events that are yet to take place.

Sometimes, your insights may be the result of your own supposition. For example, if the TV news mentions troop "exercises" near an enemy country, your dreams may make a connection, and you may dream of war. You may assume that you foresaw the future, but in reality your unconscious simply put two and two together. The really interesting predictions are the ones in which there is absolutely no way you could have known what was going to happen. For example, my wife, Jane, and I were asked to appear once a week on a television show to predict "next week's news today." Many of our insights came through dreams and included disasters that would have been impossible to anticipate by watching or reading the news. Tanker disasters, earthquakes, air crashes, and terrorist attacks are all predictions that could only be foreseen using clairvoyance.

Disasters such as the sinking of the Titanic may be foretold in dreams.

If you want to discover and improve your ability to make predictive dreams, you really should keep a dream diary. This will provide a record to prove when you had the dream and detailed information to verify your clairvoyance. I have noticed that predictive dreams tend to occur two weeks before the events take place. This was often the case in our work predicting the news for the TV show, and many other psychics have noticed this same phenomenon. Other dreams may take years to come to pass, and some, of course, never happen.

Predictive dreams may also include symbolism. As a result, the meaning of the dream will not become apparent until events unfold. For example, someone sent me a dream in which the streets of London were filled with roses that were bleeding blood. During the same week, another person wrote of seeing a heart outside Buckingham Palace.

Soon afterwards, **Diana, princess of Wales** died in a fateful car accident. To many people, she was known as the "English Rose" or the "Queen of Hearts." During the funeral, thousands threw roses at her hearse as it drove along Pall Mall; Elton John sang "Farewell Our English Rose"; and the words "Queen of Hearts" were draped across the railings of Buckingham Palace.

Remember that dreams about disaster often reflect your own emotional state and may not necessarily be about the future. For example, dreams about the end of the world or the **Apocalypse** may occur at times when you feel that your personal life is out of control. A dramatic happening in your life, such as the death of a loved one, the end of a relationship, or even hormones in adolescence, may result in end-of-the-world dreams. These dreams may be an escape mechanism to avoid dealing with a world

that has changed dramatically. In these dreams, you may find yourself alone or surrounded by strangers because in real life you feel alienated and lonely.

SIGNS, STORIES, EXPERIMENTS, AND SYMBOLS

The famous novelist Graham Greene got much of his inspiration from dreams. He kept a dream diary and drew on his dreams as inspiration for his action-packed novels. Speaking on *BBC Radio* in August 1969, he described his nightmares about the future: "I used to have a lot of atomic war dreams, which I think probably contained memories of the Blitz....I remember seeing the destruction of New York; I remember being up in Hampstead and seeing a total destruction of London with St Paul's rising up like one tooth in a toothless mouth. But for some curious reason, they were not frightening. They were interesting spectacles, and I was quite resigned at the end."

Some of Greene's dreams came true, and he described some of these in detail in his autobiography, *A Sort of Life*. "On the April night of the Titanic disaster, when I was five, I dreamt of a shipwreck," Greene wrote in his diary. "One image of the dream has remained with me for more than sixty years: a man in oilskins bent double beside a companion—way under the blow of a great wave."

Perhaps, hidden forces were warning people through dreams and coincidences of the terrible disaster that would befall the Titanic. From the very start it was prophesied that the name "Titanic" was cursed. A cockerel crowed in the daytime as she set sail—a very bad omen to sailors. As the Titanic steamed out of Southampton and past the Isle of Wight, people living along the coast stood by the shore and cheered. A Mrs. Marshall screamed and grabbed her husband Jack's arm. "It's going to sink," she said. "That ship is going to sink. Save them! Save them!" But no one listened to the hysterical ravings of a woman who appeared to have gone mad. What Mrs. Marshall did not know was that her mother had booked a passage on the Titanic.

Southampton is my hometown, and my grandmother lived her childhood in the Chapel area, where many of the ship's hands were recruited. She told me she, too, had had terrible feelings of foreboding when the Titanic set sail. She told her mother she was worried about their lodger, who was to join the crew. He was one of the few to survive the disaster, but he was deeply disturbed by what happened. Following the tragedy on April 10, 1912, Chapel was silent for weeks. Every other house in the district was grieving for a loved one. The lodger became wracked with survivor guilt and he eventually, my grandmother recalled, retired to the back room and, while the family was out, hanged himself.

Many of the people who booked a voyage on the Titanic saved their lives by clairvoyance, inexplicable "signs," or psychic dreams about the forthcoming disaster. Some canceled their journey at the last minute, including millionaire-banker J. Pierpont Morgan and businessman J. Connon Middleton, who had a recurring dream of sinking ships and drowning passengers.

Psychiatrist and parapsychologist Ian Stevenson, of the University of Virginia, researched the cases years later. He discovered 23 instances of people who had premonitions of the event—many of whose lives were saved as a result. The Society for Psychical Research still keeps the records, including an original unused ticket kept by one of those who canceled.

One of the people who saw the future was the well-known and innovative journalist William Thomas Stead. Born in 1849, he was director of the *Pall Mall Gazette* and was also seriously interested in Spiritualism. He founded two publications about psychic sciences: *Review of Reviews* and *Borderland*. In 1892, 20 years before the event, he wrote a story in which he described the awful sinking of a great liner. He also received a spirit message from an anonymous American medium who urged him not to embark on a ship, and another psychic friend, W. de Kerlor, warned him that he had a dream that involved "a catastrophe on water." Despite this, Stead disregarded his own premonitions and warnings from friends and became one of the Titanic's 1,513 victims.

See also: **Accidents**

DREAM INCUBATION (SEEDING)

Why does the eye see a thing more clearly in dreams than the imagination when awake?

LEONARDO DA VINCI, ITALIAN ARTIST

Nobody knows for certain why we dream. In *Prava naturalia*, the Greek philosopher Aristotle argued that dreams were fragments of recollections of the events of the day. Sigmund Freud believed that the purpose of dreams was to maintain sleep. Many modern theories state that dreams occur in order to prevent the emotions from "overheating."

One of the ways that dreams help to maintain your emotional equilibrium is by solving your problems. During sleep, your unconscious sorts out worries and fears by scanning all the information it can find. From this material, the subconscious weaves a dream that expresses your feelings and offers symbolic solutions to your problems. Obscure memories and half-noticed things from the day are used to build the strange imagery of dreams. I believe that the brain uses everything it can to come to a conclusion, and if it can't find the information it needs in the past and present, it looks to the future to find what it wants.

It is possible to program this, your biological computer, with a technique called "dream incubation," sometimes called "dream seeding." The word "incubate" comes from the Latin *incubare*, meaning "to lie down upon." The basic method is to tell your brain that you require an answer to a problem. Your dreams through the night and just before you wake will provide a symbolic answer to your question. Recognized as a valid technique by today's psychologists, this method stretches back to the very first dream experiments when people would sleep in the dream temples of ancient Egypt and Greece in order to receive a message from the gods.

The ancients believed that dreams provided by the temple gods related to future conditions and could also produce information about health. A simple method to incubate a dream is to write your question on a piece of paper and place it beneath your pillow. As you go to sleep, run through the question in your mind. Because dreams use a lot of visionary language, it is useful to imagine the scenario in which you want your answers to appear. For example, if the question concerns a relationship, imagine yourself with the person in question as you seed the dream. Then, relax and let the subconscious mind do the work. In the morning, your dream will contain symbols, allegories, and metaphors that express the problem. These will provide some suggestions on how to deal with the issue.

SIGNS, STORIES, EXPERIMENTS, AND SYMBOLS

There are many interesting stories about dream incubation. For example, ancient Egyptian stories tell of a man named Thothmes who slept in the desert. During the night, he received instructions from the gods saying, "Look at me, my son, Thothmes. Behold, my state is that of one in need, my whole body is going to pieces. The sands of the desert above which I stood have encroached upon me." Thothmes ordered his slaves to clear the sand, revealing the monument of the Great Sphinx, buried centuries before.

Because of this act, the Sphinx (representing the god Harmakhis) promised him that he would be the successor on Egypt's throne. The prophecy was fulfilled in 1421 B.C. when the prince ascended Egypt's throne to become Thothmes IV.

Throughout history, people have slept at sacred sites, hoping to gain help from the gods via a dream. In an unbroken tradition, Bear Butte Mountain, in the Black Hills of South Dakota, remains a vision quest site for Plains Indians. Until recently, the members of the Chumash tribe went into the hills above Santa Barbara, California, where there are hundreds of caves used to seek visions. Some of these visions have been recorded in their art and carvings.

EXTRA SENSORY PERCEPTION (ESP)

There came to me in the night a divine dream.

HOMER, GREEK POET

A psychic dream will include aspects of what the parapsychologist J.B. Rhine called Extra Sensory Perception, also referred to as ESP. Psi (from the Greek letter), psychic, and psychical are synonyms for ESP. ESP is defined as the ability to acquire information without the help of the senses.

ESP falls into four general categories:

Telepathy: This is mind-to-mind communication or a person's awareness of another's thoughts without any communication through normal perceptions.

Clairvoyance: This form of ESP includes knowledge of an object or event without the use of the known senses.

Precognition: This involves foresight; a person has foresight of another person's future thoughts or of future events.

Psychokinesis (PK): This involves mind over matter or a person's ability to influence a physical object or event by thinking about it. "Spoon bending" is an example of PK. Some parapsychologists believe that psychokinesis is not strictly extra sensory perception.

One of the best ways to test ESP for yourself is through the study of your dreams. You have dreams every night, so you have a huge amount of material with which to work. Once you learn to remember dreams and make a point of writing them down every morning, you will soon identify a few dreams that are extraordinary. They may reveal information that you could not possibly have known except by paranormal means.

SIGNS, STORIES, EXPERIMENTS, AND SYMBOLS

Many parapsychologists use Zener cards to test ESP ability. There are five kinds of cards: a star, vertical wavy lines, a plus sign, a circle, and a square. A deck of Zener cards consists of five of each symbol. In ESP tests for clairvoyance or precognition, the cards are shuffled; the subject then tries to guess the order of the cards. Another way to use these cards is to allow a sender to look at a card and then try to communicate the card telepathically to a receiver.

Packs of Zener cards are available for purchase so you can try a few experiments of your own with your friends. You can select a card and place it under your pillow at night. Your friend can attempt to guess the card in the morning. A dream may reveal the card, but since your intuition works overtime as you sleep, you may be more likely to guess the card correctly when you wake up in the morning. You will need to do the experiment over a period of many nights to ensure that your results are statistically valid and not simply the result of chance.

The Zener deck contains a total of 25 cards but only 5 different kinds of card. Thus, there is a 1 in 5 chance, or 20 percent chance, that the sender has selected any given card. A correct guess is called a "hit." If the number of hits is significantly higher than 20 percent, something other than chance is at work.

See also: **Clairvoyance, Precognition, Telepathy**

FUTURE

There is no fate!

SARAH CONNER, A CHARACTER IN *TERMINATOR 2*

Dreams that predict the future may reveal unexpected events, pitfalls, and opportunities. However, in the final analysis, you have free will and can choose your path. You may already hope or fear that certain things will happen. Your unconscious will oblige with a "psychic dream" that may be more about your own fears than things that will happen. You should maintain a sensible and discriminating attitude toward dreams and not assume that everything that is revealed is a prophecy of the future.

My own experience shows that dreams about the future have a special quality about them. You awake from the dream "knowing" that it is about the future. These dreams usually have a strangeness about them, but for me at least, they are rarely frightening or upsetting. Even disastrous events appearing in a psychic dream are experienced with calmness and sometimes with a sense of disinterest. The lack of attachment may show that the dream is not about your own anxieties and could be a prediction or premonition of real events.

If in doubt, there are a few questions you may ask about the dream to determine whether or not it is about the future:

Was the dream exceptionally vivid?

- Are there any elements that seem particularly bizarre or don't make sense?

- Does the dream include things that have never happened?

- Does the dream include people you've never met?

- Is the dream set in situations you've never before encountered?

- Is the emotional content unrelated to your own feelings?

SIGNS, STORIES, EXPERIMENTS, AND SYMBOLS

Sometimes dreams contain the strangest signs of the future, and the sleeping mind may latch on to the oddest of predictions. William Cavendish-Bentinck, the Sixth Duke of Portland, had a dream that is famous in Great Britain. While involved in preparations for the 1901 coronation procession of King Edward VII, he dreamed that the royal coach got stuck in the arch at the Horse Guards. Disturbed by the dream, he ordered the arch measured the next day. "To my astonishment," he said, "we found that the arch was nearly two feet too low to allow the coach to pass through." It had been many years since the coach had been through the arch, and over the years the level of the road had been raised by resurfacing work. The duke had the road lowered, and the procession went smoothly.

See also: **Prophecy, Serialism, Time**

GUIDES AND GURUS

I have the feeling that we have a Guardian because we serve a great cause, and that we shall have that Guardian so long as we serve that cause faithfully.

SIR WINSTON CHURCHILL, FORMER PRIME MINISTER OF GREAT BRITAIN

Could it be that during sleep we connect with the higher realms and can obtain guidance from advanced spiritual beings? Certainly, there are many famous examples of this happening. For example, St. Francis of

Assisi founded the Franciscan Order because of a dream in which Jesus spoke from the cross telling him to "go set my house in order." Similarly, it is said that just before Muhammad's birth, his father, Abdullah, dreamed of his unborn son. He saw a tree growing from his child's back. The tree climbed upward and emitted a light that spread around the world when it reached its full height. The tree represents the religion of Islam, supported by Muhammad, and the light is the wisdom of his teachings. Similarly, Muhammad also received the core teaching of Islam from a dream flight to El-Aksa (literally, "the farthest place"), an Islamic heavenly mosque in the courtyard of Allah.

Examples of holy dreams given by God, angels, saints, Bodhisattvas, or prophets can be found in all of the world's religions. Some psychical researchers believe that cases of exceptional prodigies, such as Mozart in music or Ramanujan in mathematics, provide evidence of spiritual influences working through these intuitively gifted people. It is also claimed that many of us have our own personal spirit guide that acts as the door-keeper to our soul, guiding our soul into the world at birth and helping us make the transition back to heaven at death. In addition, the guide oversees our journey through this life and may inspire us from afar.

Psychic mediums call this spirit person their guardian angel, the spirit guide, the gate-keeper, or their spirit mentor. We believe that the guides leave us to our lot because God has given us the divine blessing of free will to live our lives in our own way. However, occasionally in times of spiritual crisis, the spirit guides are permitted to interject to give us help and guidance. However, if we ask for their guidance, the request has come because of our own free will, and the guides are pleased to respond. They communicate with us through our intuition and, in particular, through psychic dreams.

SIGNS, STORIES, EXPERIMENTS, AND SYMBOLS

You can call on your "inner guide" or "inner self" using creative visualization. As you fall asleep, picture in your mind's eye a guide in the form of a man or woman. (Some people like to call on a totem animal.) Call on this inner guide to answer your questions and give you insight into your problems.

Many parapsychologists believe that these guides are aspects of an individual's unconscious and, in particular, of the male and female aspects of the psyche (animus and anima). Others believe that they are guiding spirits that communicate with us during sleep. In either case, the guides are able to see and understand things that are usually hidden from the conscious self. Practitioners who use these visualization techniques with regularity claim to experience useful insights into themselves and the world around them.

You may also call upon your inner guide to obtain a glimpse of the potential future when you ask for guidance before going to sleep. One popular method is to say, "Dear Inner Guide, I need your insight. Give me a psychic dream to answer this question: (state your question). Please give me a dream that is clear and that I can understand. In the morning, I will remember the dream easily and write it down. I will understand its meaning and follow its advice. I thank you for any direction you have to offer me about any future event."

In the morning, pay special attention to

The ancient Greeks had temples called Aesculapia where people could experience healing dreams.

any dreams you have had. They may reveal heaven-sent information about the issues in question. In addition, try to see if any of the themes and settings of the dreams reveal aspects of the nature of your spirit guide. For example, I believe one of my own spirit guides, who has spoken during séances, is Tibetan. Dreams in which he communicates usually include a cold, elevated, or mountainous setting.

See also: **Animal Spirits, Dream Incubation (Seeding)**

HEALTH AND HEALING

To heal is to make happy.

HELEN SCHUCMAN, PSYCHOLOGIST

The ancient Greek philosopher Aristotle believed that premonitory dreams of sickness could be caused by the dreamer's unconscious recognition of the symptoms. Sometimes, a treatment or sleep ritual would be devised to help incubate good dreams. This "treatment" would include abstaining from sex, meat, and drink. Aristotle postulated that dreams might be premonitions of an illness coming from within the body, where some "unconscious" mind recognized early symptoms that had not yet come to the attention of the "waking self." Clearly, the ancient Greeks had many theories about dreams that are remarkably similar to our modern concept of the unconscious mind.

Healing dreams were usually received by sleeping in the classical temples, known as Aesculapia because they were dedicated to the healing god Aeslepius. After ritual purification and ceremonial sacrifices to the local deities, the sick person spent a night in the incubation, a special part of the temple. If the gods willed it, the patient received a dream from the sons of Hypnos, the god of sleep. These were interpreted by a *therapute* who made a diagnosis. (This is the origin of our word, therapist.)

Many of theses dream temples were built on the lush Greek island of Cos, the home of the priest-healer Hippocrates. Today, we consider him to be the father of medicine because from him we get the Hippocratic oath. In its original form, this oath charged the students to examine their patients' dreams and look for symbols alluding to health and cures. The Hippocratics developed the idea that the dream was a window on illness and reflected the health of the body. Bizarre dream content was considered to be a sign of illness; on the other hand, normal content boded well for recovery and health.

The theory that dreams can diagnose illness and aid with healing is found in many cultures. For centuries, the Hindus and Chinese have used dreams to help diagnose illnesses in their advanced medical practices. They divide dreams into different classes to relate to different areas of the body, such as the heart, the lungs, and so on. Similarly, Tibetan medicine recognizes three major types of dreams: bad dreams, reflective dreams, and auspicious dreams.

Bad dreams may foretell a disaster, a serious illness, or death. Some of the images from these dreams include riding a **cat**, **monkey**, **tiger**, **fox**, or a **corpse**. Other inauspicious signs include dreams of riding naked on a **buffalo**, **horse**, or **camel**. (Each of these is a pretty chilly thing to do in Tibet.) If any of these are recurring dreams, the patient is instructed to say mantras and prayers. When the dreams stop, the patient will recover. If a healthy person has these dreams, it is considered to be a sign that an illness is imminent.

Reflective dreams deal with our emotions and worries. These dreams are interpreted in ways that are similar to Western psychology. They are for processing and clarifying everyday events.

Auspicious dreams are a sign of good fortune and recovery. These may include dreams of **holy** or **famous people**, a clear **lake**, a spotlessly white **cloth**, climbing a **mountain** or a **tree** laden with **fruit**, or receiving good **food** or **gifts**.

Tibetans believe that dreams that occur before midnight are benign and usually forgotten. However, if a dream comes just before dawn, when the mind is vivid and clear, it is especially important. As well as taking the patient's pulse and examining his or her urine, a Tibetan physician will also ask about a patient's dreams before making a diagnosis, just as ancient Greek healers did.

SIGNS, STORIES, EXPERIMENTS, AND SYMBOLS

The table below shows some of the traditional dream meanings associated with health and the body. Some superstitions need to be taken with a grain of salt. See the **Symbolism** entry for advice about the psychological way to interpret dream meanings.

See also: **Dream Incubation (Seeding)**

	Good Omen		Bad Omen
Amputation	Dreaming of losing a limb means good fortune is coming your way.	*Ankles*	To dream of the ankles of someone of the opposite sex foretells an unwise affair. Keep your socks on!
Arm	You will be in pleasant company.	*Back*	If you see someone's bare back, you will lose status.
Bandages	Bandages indicate helpful new influences.	*Baldness*	If you dream of being bald you may fall ill.
Beards	The bigger the beard, the greater the good fortune. Gray beards signify quarrels.	*Blemish*	A blemish on the body or legs indicates a scandal, but on the neck, chest, or arms it foretells success in love.
Bones	Human bones mean that money is coming, but fish bones mean ruin.	*Blindness*	Someone will deceive you. Some interpreters say it represents future poverty.
Bruise	Sorry, but you must give up your high living. Avoid overexcitement.	*Blood*	If the blood is your own, there will be family feuds. If others bleed, beware of enemies.
Death	If you die, it is a sign of a turn for the better. (I couldn't agree more.) It can also mean a birth or good news.	*Clothes*	If you have lots of clothes, you will be poor, but few clothes indicate prosperity. Soiled clothes indicate deceit.
Doctor	A doctor is a sign of general good fortune.	*Cough*	This indicates danger from fire and flood.
Eyes	Strange eyes mean a beneficial change. Seductive eyes show you will be lucky in love.	*Drowning*	Your business fortunes will be reversed.
Faces	Happy faces bring happiness and vice versa if sad. Washing your face brings troubles.	*Drugs*	You will make unwise decisions. Pills mean you have responsibilities to attend to.
Feet	These are good luck if the feet are big. Itchy feet mean travel.	*Eyelids*	Someone close to you has troubles.
Hand	If healthy and well kept, good fortune lies ahead. The reverse is true if the hand is injured.	*Eyelashes*	Secrets will be revealed. Eyebrows show that something sinister threatens you.

	Good Omen			Bad Omen	
Hospital	This is good luck if you are the visitor, but you are overtaxing yourself if you are the patient.		*Illness*	You will give into temptations that may cause problems.	
Injury	Your talents will be recognized.		*Invalid*	Your success will be delayed.	
Mouth	You will gain success if you watch your words.		*Itch*	You worry too much.	
Neck	This represents financial success, but problems lie ahead if the neck is broken.		*Nose*	A nose is usually a bad sign, particularly if it is running or sore. It is good luck if you blow your nose.	
Nurse	This is a superstition for family unity.		*Paralysis*	You have inner conflicts.	
X-ray	An X-ray is an oracle that indicates good health.		*Teeth*	If these are painful or damaged, there will be ill luck. Healthy or false teeth mean great good fortune.	

HYPNAGOGIC AND HYPNOPOMPIC DREAMS

Not all lucid dreams are useful, but they all have a sense of wonder about them. If you must sleep through a third of your life, why should you sleep through your dreams, too?

STEPHEN LABERGE, PSYCHOLOGIST

The philosopher Ouspensky became interested in the occult because of his childhood interest in the dream visions that he had while apparently wide-awake. Many of these visions occurred as he was falling asleep or immediately on waking.

Ouspensky was experiencing the extraordinary state of consciousness that psychologists call hypnagogic and hypnopompic dreaming that occurs at the point between waking and sleep. Hypnagogic imagery may occur as you are falling to sleep, and hypnopompic imagery may occur on waking. People also report auditory, visual, kinesthetic, and tactile hallucinations as well as floating sensations and out-of-body experiences.

If you have ever experienced this strange state of awareness, you will know that the visions are remarkable and may include vivid pictures and scenes that are astonishing in their clarity. My experiences with this phenomenon during my teens inspired me to seriously consider painting as a career in order to capture some of the extraordinary images I was seeing.

The hypnagogic and hypnopompic states happen when you are right on the brink between being awake and being asleep. They are sometimes accompanied by sleep paralysis and sometimes by frightening images and a feeling of helplessness, as if you are under a psychic **attack** by **demons**. On the other hand, I have been a hypnagogic dreamer all my life, and I have never had any unpleasant experiences or paralysis during this state. Indeed, I have always found this state of consciousness to be extremely inspiring and one that can be a stepping-stone to all sorts of psychic experiences.

Hypnagogic dreaming can be a means to trigger out-of-body travel, and it can also be used to induce lucid dreams. Although the images in a hypnagogic dream are very hard to recall afterward, I have used this state to look into the future. If the stream of awareness is targeted to a specific subject, such as what tomorrow's newspaper headline will be, I have found that these dreams sometimes reveal images relating to the future.

SIGNS, STORIES, EXPERIMENTS, AND SYMBOLS

Inducing hypnagogic dreaming requires you to remain wakeful as you fall to sleep. Some people do this by drinking a lot of coffee before retiring because this keeps the mind active as the dream state kicks in. Chocolate will also induce wakefulness as it contains theobromine, which is similar in effect to caffeine.

Some authorities recommend keeping the mind active by imagining doing something that involves audible and tactile sensations. For example, imagining driving a car can help you retain a conscious state. Visualize the car and the road, hear the engine and the radio, and feel the steering wheel. This will help you retain your attention as sleep creeps up on you.

I have found that these artificial methods are not necessary once you establish the habit of hypnagogic dreaming. You only need to remain alert as your brain drifts toward sleep. You can retain wakefulness by thinking of mathematical problems or word games. This stops the logical mind from falling into the abstract thinking that accompanies sleep and maintains wakefulness.

If you can maintain wakefulness as you hover at the edge of sleep, you will start to see images in your mind's eye. Sometimes, I also see them as if they are happening behind my actual eyes, as if they are being projected onto my eyelids. In most instances though, the imagery appears as if floating in the space in front of you.

Because some of the images may be frightening, you should remember that this is a hypnotic state; don't become too involved with the image. I have found that maintaining a transcendent state, like an observer, helps to increase the intensity of the images. Try focusing on an image and asking yourself questions about it. Can you see the colors more clearly? What is its texture? Perhaps you can also induce sounds and smells associated with the images you see. I have found that the more you focus your senses on the images you see, the more "real" they become.

You may see landscapes, faces, and all sorts of strange imagery. I have had instances where the images have turned into cartoon animations, and I have witnessed incredible displays of imagery over which I have no conscious control. I often question where all this extraordinary imagery comes from because I could never dream up such images in a million years!

The benefit of this state is that it gives you access to the astonishing creativity that you have but have never tapped into in waking life. When you experience this state, you may wonder at the potential you have to create imagery. You may find the experience creatively inspiring. The state may also help you to begin lucid dreaming and open your powers of ESP.

See also: **Lucid Dreams**

INTUITION

Imagination is the eye of the soul.

JOSEPH JOUBERT, FRENCH PHILOSOPHER

Intuition often reveals itself in dreams. It is at work while you sleep and can sometimes offer solutions to problems through dreams. During the day, your unconscious mind may have noticed something about a person or a situation and will bring this to your attention through a dream. For example, you meet a friend during the day. That evening, you have a dream about that person being ill. You noticed nothing wrong with the person during the day. However, your unconscious may have observed telltale signs of an illness. The tone of the complexion, an imperceptible odor, or a slight quiver in the voice could all be subtle signals unconsciously observed and then brought to your attention during sleep when intuition is allowed to function. In many cases, your intuition gives an answer to a problem or produces information that is impossible for it to know. The most obvious of these occurs when we have an intuitive glimpse of the future.

Some of the greatest minds trusted their intuition to help them solve difficult intellectual problems. The inventor Thomas Edison took catnaps while working. He was convinced that some of his best inventions came to him while sleeping. Sometimes, the best way to deal with a problem or to solve a problem is to simply "sleep on it." During the day, the conscious, rational mind is in complete control of your life, and you do things because you have a logical reason for behaving in such a way. However at night, the intuition breaks through the stranglehold of reason and forces an idea upon you that you could never have arrived at by logical thought alone. Intuition is the source of many great ideas that arise from the unconscious and sometimes by paranormal means.

Many great inventions are the result of dream intuition. For example, the sewing machine owes its invention to a dream. Elias Howe was stuck for a solution for a working model. One night, he dreamed that a savage king ordered him to invent a sewing machine. When Howe said that he had tried but couldn't, the whole tribe raised their spears to kill him. Just before the fateful moment, Howe noticed that each spear had a hole in it immediately above the point. This was the vital clue needed for the commercial perfection of the sewing machine.

Atomic physics owes one of its fundamental discoveries to the intuitive insight of a dream. Neils Bohr was trying to understand the nature of the atom. One night, he dreamed of a sun composed of burning gasses. Planets attached to fine threads were orbiting it. When he awoke, he realized that this was the solution to his puzzle. It explained the structure of the atom and heralded the birth of atomic physics.

Of course, there are many examples of spontaneous insight resulting from intuition. This "eureka" effect has influenced inventors, generals, artists, scientists, and people from just about every profession. The truth is that the unconscious is like an incredible inner computer that continues solving problems for you in the background of your normal awareness. When it has done its work, the answers pop into your head.

In 1765, the composer Giuseppe Tartini dreamed that he made a pact with the devil and handed him his violin. "I found myself handing him my violin to see if he might manage some pretty tunes; but imagine my astonishment when I heard a sonata so unusual and so beautiful, performed with such mastery and intelligence, on a level I had never before conceived was possible! I was so overcome that I stopped breathing and awoke gasping. Immediately I seized my violin, hoping to recall some shred of what I had just heard, but in vain. The piece I then composed is without doubt my best, and I still call it the *Devil's Sonata*, but it falls so far short of the one that stunned me that I would have smashed my violin and given up music forever if I could but possess it."

Whether the *Devil's Sonata* was received from the unconscious mind or from the **devil** is subject to debate.

JOURNEYS

When you come to a fork in the road, take it.

IRISH SAYING

The storytelling quality of dreams is reflected in mythology, which was the psychology of its time. Some of the most compelling myths are those that tell of mystical journeys, because they express the journey of the self toward wholeness. The treasure of self-realization is the hero's reward once he triumphs over adversity. This inner journey is expressed in myths such as the travels of Odysseus, Jason's search for the Golden Fleece, Gilgamesh's journey to find immortality, and in modern myths such as *Star Wars* and *The Lord of the Rings*.

I include the theme of journeys as a psychic dream because many people who are experiencing these are on a spiritual quest toward self-knowledge. Patanjali, the author of the ancient Yoga Sutras, explains that psychic powers and psychic dreams should not be the goal of the spiritual seeker. These are what he calls siddhis, powers that develop naturally as the adept moves toward divine insight. When a person takes the spiritual journey toward enlightenment, these powers arise spontaneously, but they are not the ultimate goal. In fact, they can become a trap for some people because psychic powers may strengthen their sense of self-importance and prevent the final union with the divine state. Similarly in Western myths, the hero may triumph throughout his journey but eventually fall victim to his own egotism (known as hubris).

The act of dreaming is a journey into the center of yourself. The symbols of these dreams usually show the stages of your development. Nonetheless, journey dreams may also represent a period of time and be a symbol for the journey into the future. The things you see along the road may represent a sequence in time. The events that will happen soon may be shown at the start of the journey and distant forecasts toward its completion. But as with all journeys, there are many paths you may take to get to the same goal. If your dream shows worrisome events ahead, it may also show another direction to go so that you may avoid pitfalls. Your dream may not be predicting events but may be offering potential pathways to success.

Being on a journey in dreams often points to a spiritual quest of self-discovery.

SIGNS, STORIES, EXPERIMENTS, AND SYMBOLS

The table below shows some of the traditional dream meanings associated with journeys and dreams that allegedly predict a journey. Some superstitions need to be taken with a grain of salt. See the **Symbolism** entry for advice about the psychological way to interpret dream meanings.

Good Travel Omen		Bad Travel Omen	
Abroad	If you dream of traveling abroad, enemies will be overcome.	Boat	If it sinks, so will your hopes. A boat represents your life and shows what is happening: smooth sailing, becalmed, etc.
Acting	If you are acting, this is a sign of successful journeys.	Bridge	This is a good omen if you pass over it, but it is a bad omen if you pass under it.
Adventure	To dream of setting out on an adventure augurs good fortune.	Briefcase	If it is new, it shows an unsuccessful business trip. Old briefcases foretell success.
Atlas	If you dream of reading an atlas, you will travel soon.	Bus	This journey presages difficult times ahead.
Bag	A leather bag indicates travel.	Cabin	Domestic troubles are ahead if you dream of being in a ship's cabin.
Bunion	A traveler will return home soon. Itching feet also predict travel.	Cargo	If the cargo drops, you will lose money. Loading a ship's cargo indicates travel over a short distance.
Cab	Travel to a foreign country will bring wealth. If you journey at night, an affair will be exposed.	Cart	A dream of traveling by cart shows that someone is assassinating your good character.
Camel	To travel by camel brings love and riches.	Chariot	To journey by chariot foretells poverty.
Drawbridge	You will have an unexpected journey.	Comet	This is a warning of natural disasters. Do not travel.
East	To travel east shows a pilgrimage.	Desert	A journey in the desert indicates dangers and difficulties ahead.
Emigration	You will receive a letter or a present from a good friend.	Driving	Driving shows you have nasty habits and poor personal hygiene. Caution with money is advised.
Farewell	Saying farewell shows that your lover or friend is true.	Feet	If you dream of having an extra foot, you may become ill soon.
Flamingo	You will have success with all foreign travel if the bird is flying.	Field	Walking in a field shows your life will be monotonous.
Flatulence	An unexpected trip is foreseen. This can also predict arguments.	Flying	Dreaming of flying backward is a bad omen for sailors.
Gondola	Traveling in a gondola indicates others will work on your behalf.	Grotto	This is a warning of perilous journeys. Others say it may mean a lightening of burdens.
Hiccup	This predicts travel for you soon.	Head	If your head is turned back to front, emigrate because you have many enemies.
Hummingbird	You will have business success in a foreign country.	Hill	Traveling over hills shows you will have many obstacles to overcome.

	Good Travel Omen		Bad Travel Omen
Jail	You could make money as a traveler or traveling salesman.	Island	A journey to an island foretells a broken relationship.
Jetty	Soon you will travel to a foreign country.	Knapsack	If it is empty, hard times are ahead. If it is full, you will have good fortune.
Jug	To drink out of a jug shows a journey. The bigger the jug, the longer the journey.	Landing	Landing from a boat is not a good omen for sailors and merchants.
Kilt	You will take an unexpected trip.	Lighthouse	You will be forced to take a journey.
Lifeboat	You may be closely connected to or marry a seafaring person.	Limping	You will have to journey on foot. Check the car for problems.
Map	You will travel to meet a stranger. Brightly colored maps show a happy journey.	Marsh	To journey through a marsh bodes misfortune. However, if you dream of freeing yourself, you will eventually succeed.
Navigation	Successful sailing shows success in your affairs.	Navy	If you dream of joining the navy, you will have troubles in love.
Ocean	It is lucky to dream of the ocean if you are about to go on a journey.	Orient	Dreams set in the Orient tell of romantic happiness that will not last.
Pilgrim	If you see a traveling pilgrim, it foretells success for the future.	Packing	To dream of packing shows that you will rarely travel for pleasure.
Pirate	Exciting journeys lie ahead, but beware of deceit from a friend.	Pendulum	Bad news means you may have to travel.
Rainbow	You will experience financial success, particularly with foreign trade.	Quail	Someone traveling from afar will bring bad news.
Raspberry	You will hear news of a happy marriage overseas.	Raft	You will be forced to take a journey.
Roads	Straight roads are good luck; crooked roads presage misfortune.	Rescue	Avoid all travel. This is a bad omen.
Sailing	If the sea is calm, you will have a happy life. Rough seas predict wealth.	Rudder	Do not travel. You will have to return because of indecision.
Sheep	Sailors believe that to dream of sheep means you will have a happy voyage, and your lover will be true.	Shaving	If a sailor dreams of shaving, it means there will be stormy weather.
Star	You will have advantage through travel if this is seen in a clear sky.	Shipwreck	You have false friends.
Thigh	If you dream of having big thighs, you will have a happy voyage.	Train	Fast trains mean you should delay long journeys.
View	Journeying through beautiful scenery presages a fortunate future.	Valley	Traveling through a valley signifies temporary sickness.
Voyage	This can mean messages from a distance are on their way to you.	Wandering	Aimless wandering is a sign that trouble is coming soon.
Wayfarer	Meeting a wayfarer means you will make a new friend soon.	Wheel	Broken wheels foretell dangerous or delayed journeys.
Yacht	This indicates financial improvements and money luck.	Zoo	You will meet new people in a faraway place.

LUCID DREAMS

While we are asleep in this world, we are awake in another one.

SALVADOR DALI, PAINTER

Have you ever had the experience of waking up in a dream while it is still taking place? One moment you are happily dreaming, then suddenly you dream of saying, "Hey this is a dream! I'm asleep!" If you have managed to remain asleep after you have realized you are dreaming, you may also have noticed that it is possible to control your dream. You may decide to rewind it and go back to an enjoyable part of the dream, or you may be able to influence the conclusion of a dream and turn it into a happy ending. Waking up in a dream as it is taking place is called lucid dreaming. The term was first coined by Frederik van Eeden, who used the word "lucid" in the sense of mental clarity.

A lucid dream normally arises in the midst of a dream when you realize that you are dreaming. An impossible occurrence in the dream, such as having superhuman powers, may trigger this awareness.

Sometimes, a lucid dream happens for no apparent reason. The level of lucidity can vary greatly. At the best level, you are aware that everything you are experiencing in the dream is occurring in your mind, and you never have any sense of danger or alarm. In a high-level lucid dream, you are aware that you are safe and will awaken shortly. In a low-level lucid dream, you may be aware to an extent that you are dreaming, but you are not aware enough to radically alter the content or understand that you are actually in bed.

Lucid dreaming is a very useful technique to help overcome problems. For example, if you have persistent dreams of **being chased**, you may decide, when you have control of the dream, to turn and face your attacker. In this way, you are able to unmask what it is that is troubling you. Instead of running from your problems, you will have started to address them. Such lucid dream techniques may help you build your self-confidence. You can also use lucid dreams to increase your skills or creativity. For example, the novelist Graham Greene would often turn to dreams to help him plan his books. Greene's widow, Viviene, said that some of the stories "came to him in dreams. He was interested in them from his early youth when he was being analyzed." Some of Greene's dreams contained prophecies. He foresaw the sinking of the *Titanic* (see **Disasters**) and is on record as foretelling the death of General Omar Torrijos, the Panamanian president, who died in a plane crash in 1979.

Lucid dreams are a fascinating state of consciousness that allow you to control your dreams and experience anything imaginable. Often dreams about the dead are accompanied by lucidity in the dream, indicating perhaps that this is a real experience and not your imagination. Similarly, some psychics consider lucid dreams to be the stepping-stone to an out-of-body experience (OBE) which can enable the dreamer to visit other places in this world and other dimensions.

Lucid dreaming enables you to have more control over your emotions, creativity, and spiritual powers, but don't take things too far. If you constantly direct dream characters and alter dream landscapes without exploring the symbolic nature of your dreams, you may be suppressing your unconscious needs. Therefore, you need to allow time for "free dreaming" so that symbolic messages from your unconscious are given expression.

SIGNS, STORIES, EXPERIMENTS, AND SYMBOLS

As I have explained, dreams about flying and other extraordinary feats are an indication that your dream may be on the point of becoming lucid. However, these themes also have important symbolic meanings that reveal things about yourself and the way you are feeling.

Flying: To dream of flying may represent an escape from something that has been troubling you. It may show liberation from an emotional or material problem or simply show a release of tension. It is usually a pleasant experience. Freud claimed that flying dreams were symbolic of the pleasure associated with the release of sexual tension. Flying can also represent having ambitions that are too high; and just like Icarus in the Greek myth, you may take a tumble if you set your sights too high. According to the old dream oracles, dreaming of flying high predicts marital troubles. Flying low is a prophecy of temporary sickness, and flying over ruins shows bad luck. White wings are lucky, but black wings foretell of disaster.

Jumping: Often, a dream about being able to make huge jumps, like Spiderman in the comic books, triggers a lucid dream. As a symbol, this may represent your feelings about making sudden advancements in your life. A romance may be going well, or you may have had a promotion. It may also be a pun to say be "one jump ahead" of the competition. Traditional prophecies associated with jumping and **leaping** indicate that you will succeed in any endeavor, but if you jump and fall then things will turn out for the worse. Disappointments in love are forecast if you jump down a wall.

Striding: Dreams of flying may be preceded by a dream in which you can take massive steps and eventually take off into the air. Strange, **superhuman** abilities often appear in a dream that is about to turn lucid. Striding off course can also be a symbol to express your feelings about taking "great strides" in life. You may be advancing in your career, in a relationship, or with a project of some kind. Dream oracles say that to **run** alone indicates that you will outstrip your friends; to run with others indicates a forthcoming festivity. If you run or **walk** through unpleasant scenery, forthcoming events will be troublesome. The reverse is true if the **landscape** is pleasant or beautiful.

See also: **Clairvoyance, Death and Dying, Out-of-Body Experiences (OBEs), Telepathy, Wicca and Witchcraft**

LUCK

Life is not holding a good hand;
Life is playing a poor hand well.

DANISH PROVERB

A great deal of superstition surrounds dreams and their ability to forecast good or bad luck. Folklore says that clean or **shiny** objects are lucky omens, but **dirty or dull** objects bring bad luck. Dreams of **ascending** indicate success, but dreams of **descending** show failure. Most **successful** efforts in a dream are a sign of good luck; on the other hand, **failure** in a dream indicates failure in

Good Luck		Bad Luck	
Alarm	Alarm bells mean business profits.	*Abdomen*	An exposed abdomen is a warning to beware of treachery.
Ambulance	Tradition has it that your hopes will be fulfilled.	*Alligator*	These snappy creatures indicate that you have hidden enemies.
Baker	If you dream of a baker, your fortunes will improve.	*Artist*	This means time is being wasted. Looks like the ancients didn't value art either.
Barber	To dream of a barber shows success after difficulties.	*Author*	Promotion is possible, but don't lend money.
Beggar	This indicates you will be helped. Plan for success.	*Bacchus*	To dream of the Roman god of wine foretells a time of very hard work.
Bench	Important money news is on its way.	*Battles*	These can indicate trouble in many aspects of your life.
Berries	A sign of advancement and promotion.	*Bishop*	Bad news is coming.
Bicycle	Unexpected help comes your way.	*Blunder*	This is a contrary dream of unexpected career success. Bad if you're not ready.

real life. If you are not on good terms with your **family,** dreaming about them pertains to business advancement. If relations are unpleasant, then the reverse is foretold.

To complicate things, folklore also includes the rule of contrary and opposites. In other words, some dreams mean the opposite of what they appear to mean. For example, dreaming of a **death** often means a rebirth of some sort, such as a marriage or the start of a new career. Interwoven with this system are traditional symbols of good luck, such as lucky or unlucky buildings, ships, roads, plays, and times of day. In addition to all of this, we have inherited dream superstitions from the Romans and others. It isn't hard to see that the meaning of lucky or unlucky dreams can sometimes be a little hard to unravel. If you look up the lucky meaning for a dream in a number of directories, you will discover that what is classified as lucky in one tradition is considered unlucky in another. The secret is to keep looking so that you will eventually find a lucky meaning for just about every dream.

Some psychologists have argued that a belief that you are lucky actually helps you to become more successful. People who believe they are lucky are generally more confident in facing challenges, while those who believe they are unlucky are less sure of their abilities and tend to underachieve.

SIGNS, STORIES, EXPERIMENTS, AND SYMBOLS

Superstition gives us a number of dream interpretations about luck themes. Some of the interpretations of these dreams are contrary and could go either way. The table below shows some of the traditional dream meanings associated with luck and destiny. I have also included here some of the meanings for the people, such as bakers, sailors, and so on, that may appear in your dreams. See the **Symbolism** entry for advice about the psychological way to interpret dream meanings.

Good Luck		Bad Luck	
Birth	This indicates achievement. To dream of your own birth is a good sign for someone in need of advancement.	Boss	If you are friendly to your boss, it is a sign that your laziness will be reprimanded.
Burglar	Your finances will improve. (How is not explained in the old oracles.)	Briefcase	There will only be success if the case is old and battered. Otherwise, this is a sign of misfortune.
Call	If someone calls your name, there will be important news.	Cleaning	Be careful of illegal deals.
Children	These are a traditional sign of success in business and career, particularly if they are healthy and fair.	Clock	You are wasting time. Try to stay awake during job interviews.
Chimney	The taller the chimney, the greater your achievements.	Committee	Problems and upheavals are ahead.
Coffee	There will be good news soon.	Cushions	You must reduce your expenditures.
Dawn	Watch out for a lucky new opportunity.	Dagger	Beware of treachery from supposed friends.
Dragon	Someone in authority may help you find success.	Dam	Impulsive actions may lead to a failure.
Earth	This is a sign of business profits.	Earwig	Beware of gossip.
Embarrassment	This indicates success so long as you stick to your decisions.	Employment	Reverse the dream. A job offer indicates failure and shows possible unemployment.
Escape	You are moving toward success.	Entombment	Do not put yourself forward. Let others sing your praises.
Feathers	You will be very popular with your colleagues at work.	Factory	This is an indication of a potential health problem.
Flag	New opportunities are on their way.	Failure	This is a contrary dream indicating glorious success in everything you do.
Floor	New ventures will be successful.	Famous	You will be demoted. Watch out!
Footsteps	Learning a new skill will be to your advantage.	Ferret	Be careful what you say if you uncover clandestine deals.
Furniture	Good prospects for you if the furniture is in good condition. Damaged furniture warns of trouble.	Flatulence	Do not argue with superiors or make a stink about conditions. You will be the one who loses out.
Gangway	Your career is going through a necessary period of transition. Luck comes later.	Garnet	You will work hard for very little reward. Sound familiar?
Gloves	Your self-reliance brings success. Gloves are lucky if you are starting a self-employed venture.	Gun	You will be wronged in some way. If looking for work, do not ask at inter-views if the company has a policy regarding concealed weapons.
Hammer	This is a sign of achievement. You can start that trust fund.	Helmet	There will be problems due to lack of organization.
Handcuffs	Success and good luck will be with you very soon.	Hiding	If you are hiding, you must own up to a mistake.

Good Luck		Bad Luck	
Hearse	Some of your work responsibilities will be lightened.	Hive	Complete dangerous undertakings quickly, or they will overrun you.
Horse	Expect a promotion. You'll have exceptional luck if the horse is being shod.	Hoax	You may be called before the boss and reprimanded.
Hunger	Improvements are coming. You'll enjoy luck with money and a salary increase.	Holly	There will be arguments.
Ice	A long-delayed opportunity will eventually come to you.	Income	To dream of a big income is a sign of failure.
Job	Great good luck if you are fired in your dream.	Javelin	You are held back at work. Extend your career ambitions.
Lion	The lion is a symbol of advancement. This is a good dream to have if you are seeking promotion.	Knife	This is a sign of injustice. You'll experience bad luck with partnerships.
Lunatic	Good news and a new working environment await you.	Medium	If you meet a medium in your dream, you will be misguided.
Machinery	If running well, it indicates success. If broken, you'll have employment problems.	Mill	You may lose your job, but you will inherit a fortune.
Magnet	This foretells personal success and business security.	Napkin	Unpleasant news is coming. Read the small print.
Nudity	If you are nude in a public place, you will find success. If others are nude, beware of deceit.	Orders	If you give them, you will be demoted. If you receive them, you will advance.
Office	Dreams about the office show good luck in personal relationships.	Pendulum	An unexpected (and perhaps unwanted) change of routine is coming.
Pigs	These animals indicate big troubles at home, but there will be success at work.	Puppets	Management is manipulating you.
Prize	To be given a prize shows you will be honored.	Raft	You may be forced to relocate or change jobs.
Quarrel	At work or home, there will be peace and harmony.	Rest room	You will have disagreements with a work colleague.
Signature	A signature is usually taken as a sign of job security.	Snow	This indicates problems at first, but you will progress in the long term.
Towel	If clean, it means you'll have improvements in your life.	Table	Improvements are coming, but great hard work foreseen.
Uniform	You will enjoy your work.	Unicorn	A liar may harm your reputation.
Warden	A prison warden indicates you will have a long and pleasant vacation.	Vest	There will be hostility from your colleagues.
Wool	To buy or sell wool augurs success in any trade or sales job.	Wages	Be aware that there are thieves near you.
Yolk	To beat eggs in a dream shows success is coming to you.	Yacht	Trouble lies ahead if you are putting work before pleasure.
Zinc	Luck and opportunities may lie overseas.	Zeppelin	This indicates that you are overly ambitious and may tumble.

MONEY

For I did dream of money-bags tonight.

WILLIAM SHAKESPEARE, PLAYWRIGHT

Your dreams will try to solve many of your everyday problems. Of course, this includes how to sort out your personal finances. Sometimes, your dreams can give you direct insights into your money problems and show you ways to find good fortune.

As with all apparently prophetic dreams, you'll need to decide if a dream about money is about psychological issues. For example, dreaming of a lack of money can symbolize a lack of the abilities or qualifications needed to achieve some desired goal. **Hoarding** money can be a symbol of selfishness, whereas to dream of **sharing** money can symbolize magnanimity. Dreams about finding treasure may be an allegory, describing a hidden part of you, such as a talent or hitherto unfulfilled ambitions.

I have had some interesting letters from people who have dreamed about a quick fix solution to solve their finances. For example, one dreamer said, "The night before I went to a racecourse, I dreamed of the winning horse. I had never visited a racecourse before. Talk about beginner's luck! Not only did I know what horse would win, but I also was shown that it would be the second race of the evening. I placed a bet on the horse I'd dreamed about. Incredibly, it came in at odds of 8 to 1. I won $62, and I wish now that I had trusted my dream and put more on!"

This case is an exception. I have noticed that most of the dreams people have about money have an infuriating twist. A typical instance of this is in a letter from a man who wrote, "I dreamed I saw a group of horses with jockeys, but the horses were standing or wandering about while the five or so jockeys were either lying on the ground or getting to their feet. I saw that the fence in front of them was broken down, and I saw a lone horse shoot through the gap. I saw a glimpse of the winning post, and I heard a cry go out, 'The winner is the 50-to-1 outsider!'

"Although I'm not usually a gambler, I looked at the morning paper, went straight down to the bookies, and placed a bet on the only two horses with 50-to-1 odds. The exact event in my dream came true, and Foinavon won at 50-to-1. However, it wasn't the horse I'd bet on. Unfortunately, there were three, not two horses, with 50-to-1 odds."

Sometimes, dreams about the future may come from a spiritual source; such a dream cannot be used for personal financial gain. Many psychic mediums believe that psychic powers cannot be used to bring benefit to oneself. If this were not the case, psychics would win the lotto every week! An interesting example of this happened to Uri Geller, the spoon-bending psychic. On October 30, 1978, the British newspaper *The Daily Mirror* published a three-page article about Geller. In particular, it included an account of a gambling session he played in at the Victoria Sporting Club. By the end of the evening, he had won several thousand pounds. The next day, Uri Geller reported that he could hear an angry voice in his head telling him not to use his powers like that. He never gambled again.

Perhaps psychic powers are not to be used for monetary gain. For that reason they may

Dreams of gambling and money may indicate financial success.

not always include the financial insights you may desire. My own experience has shown that sometimes dreams have given me important monetary or business insights. I have acted on these dreams and benefited. These dreams have come spontaneously and at times when I needed guidance. My belief is that psychic dreams about money come to us when our intent is correct and at a time when our spiritual path can be eased by a limited material gain.

The table below shows some of the traditional dream meanings associated with **money** and **wealth**. Some superstitions need to be taken with a grain of salt. See the **Symbolism** entry for advice about the psychological way to interpret dream meanings.

Financial Success		Financial Failure	
Abandonment	Your problems will end.	*Abbey*	Bad luck if seen at night, but success if seen during the day.
Acorn	Good fortune and happiness are coming your way.	*Accountant*	Guard your money.
Airplane	This indicates good financial news.	*Anchor*	Sorry, you will not join the navy. Superstition says you need to economize.
Apron	You'll experience financial improvement.	*Antiques*	Buying antiques forecasts an inheritance, but it indicates trouble with loans if you dream of selling them.
Arial	You will receive extra money.	*Ashes*	Financial setbacks occur unless they come from a cremation, which indicates an inheritance.
Beans	To dream of cooking beans brings increased income.	*Bag*	A paper bag indicates money troubles; cloth indicates success.
Burning	You can look forward to increasing prosperity. If a house burns down, it indicates riches and an inheritance.	*Button*	If you dream of losing a button, you will seriously overspend. If it is new, you will experience good fortune.
Cattle	Old superstitions say that to dream of cattle brings prosperity.	*Counterfeit*	Dreaming of counterfeit money brings bad health.
Cheese	To dream of eating cheese brings luck in both love and money. If the cheese is grated, the money will be substantial.	*Court*	Dreaming of court brings financial setbacks. If you give evidence, there will be major financial problems.
Coins	The smaller the coin, the more money is coming to you.	*Embezzlement*	Be careful; it may happen in real life.
Cooking	Money is coming, particularly if you dream of cooking soup.	*Entrails*	If a rich man dreams of eating his own entrails, it heralds financial misfortune. Good luck for the rest of us though.
Crime	If you commit a crime, money is on the way.	*Eskimo*	Your application for a loan will be unsuccessful.
Dish	A full dish brings luck at gambling.	*Food*	Tasting food signals loss of income.

Financial Success		Financial Failure	
Evergreens	You'll have success with money. This can also mean friendship.	Gambling	If you win in the dream, you will loose in real life and vice versa.
Fish	If you catch a fish in a dream, your fortunes will soon improve.	Giggling	What you lose in money you make up for in love.
Floating	This is a sign of easily gained prosperity.	Gold	Guard your possessions. This can also mean wealth you never enjoy.
Food	To dream of selling food brings good fortune.	Hay	Money troubles lie ahead if the hay is dry. The reverse is true if it is wet.
Invitation	You will soon have an opportunity to make money.	Income	Reverse this dream. A large income means failure. Poverty spells riches.
Ivy	You'll enjoy wealth and happiness. It can also mean a faithful partner.	Jungle	Disastrous financial entanglements lie ahead.
Kettle	A kettle brings good luck and financial success if it is boiling. If it is dry, you face misfortune.	Lace	Beware of extravagance. Tying shoelaces shows wealth in old age.
Log	This foretells an unexpected windfall.	Needle	Bad luck and loss are indicated, but rewards can come from hard work.
Meat	You will have success in business ventures.	Nest	If there are no eggs, you will marry someone poor.
Money	This is good fortune. To pay money indicates the birth of a son.	Owl	A very bad omen for business. Stay in bed.
Onion	Your finances will improve if you dream of eating raw onions.	Perjury	You deserve the bad luck that is coming to you.
Pearls	You'll attain prosperity through hard work. These can also foretell news of illness.	Quartz	Forget the New Age remedies. Dreaming of quartz means someone will cheat you.
Quilt	Easy money comes your way.	Raffle	You do not deserve your success.
Rabbits	These are a sign of changes that lead to financial success.	Sand	Beware of enemies who may steal your success.
Salt	You will be successful in everything you undertake. Some say salt warns of enemies.	Swamps	Your finances will sink. These are generally considered to be bad luck in relation to all money issues.
Silver	You'll have good luck with money.	Till	An empty till warns of unscrupulous employers.
Swimming	This is a sign of good fortune and better times ahead.	Trumpet	Tradesmen playing trumpets signify ruin and business liquidation.
Telephone	An invention earns you a fortune.	Twins	You will work forever and may never retire.
Toad	To fight a toad brings financial success.	Vegetables	Most vegetable dreams indicate work that goes unpaid.
Tools	These are portents of financial rewards.	Wages	Lock your doors; this foretells a robbery.
Umbrella	If you dream of losing one, you will receive an unexpected gift.	Writing	Beware of bad financial advice. Change your accountant.

MUTUAL DREAMS

Goodnight, Irene, Goodnight, Irene,
I'll see you in my dreams.

FROM "GOODNIGHT, IRENE," SONG WRITTEN
BY HUDDIE LEDBETTER AND JOHN A. LOMAZ

A mutual dream is a special case of telepathy in which two people meet in a dream and communicate with each other in some way in their separate worlds. Mutual dreams may include dreams in which two or more dreamers meet each other. Sometimes, these may take the form of dream romances, shared nightmares, out-of-body experiences, and lucid meetings. Rarer are "meshing dreams," in which people view the world from another's perspective, actually sharing the same dream experience but seeing and feeling the situation from the other person's point of view.

The strength of the emotional link is an important factor in mutual dreams. Telepathy tends to work well between people who like each other. It is most often experienced between people who love each other. You are likely to share the same dreams with family, close friends, and your partner. A shared dream may even mean you have met your **soulmate.**

Your mutual dream may not be exactly the same in every detail, but there are usually striking similarities. If you intend to test these dreams for their validity, you and the person who has been having similar dreams must write down your dreams every night. This will give you some proof that you shared the same or very similar dream material. Your dreams may include similar settings or similar emotional themes. These dreams are likely to include vivid **colors** and may feel as if they are out of place with other dreams from that night or from the recent past. You may find that you both dream of the same places or people and that you may say the same words in your dream. You may become aware of meeting in your dream as it is taking place. This will allow you to gain even more control over the experience, particularly if both of you are skilled in lucid dreaming. There is no experience as intimate as directly sharing a dream with someone you love.

SIGNS, STORIES, EXPERIMENTS, AND SYMBOLS

I set up an interesting dream telepathy experiment on my Internet Web site to test the signs of mutual dreams. I asked visitors to my chatroom classes to travel to my home in their dreams and tell me what objects I had placed on the top of my television set. The intention was to see if two or more people could share the same dream. As I went to sleep, I thought about the objects on the TV and attempted to send thoughts about them to my students. In the next online class, many of the participants came very close to the target, and some had very similar dreams. Some of them believed they saw each other in their dreams. One visitor's dream achieved a direct hit and featured all three of the objects I had placed on the TV: a teddy bear, a hat, and a pair of scissors.

NATURE

Tongues in trees, books in the running brooks,
sermons in stones, and good in everything.

WILLIAM SHAKESPEARE, PLAYWRIGHT

Dreams about nature, and particularly those that predicted the weather, were of great importance to rural people whose

Some dreams can be omens of powerful natural events.

livelihood depended on the success of their agriculture. The ancients believed that dreams provided insight into the divine influences that determined the weather. In some parts of the world, sacrifices and rituals are still undertaken to appease the gods in the hope that this will persuade them to improve the weather.

Weather lore has its origin in observations of nature and the behavior of animals. For example, a red sky at night shows there is little moisture in the air to the west, so you can expect sun the next day. Bad weather is predicted from cows and horses sitting, seagulls flying inland, house martins flying low, cats sneezing, ants seeking shelter, and bees remaining in their hive. Similarly, if oak trees produce leaves before ash trees, the summer will be good. If the groundhog emerges from its burrow on Groundhog Day (February 2nd) and doesn't see its shadow, it will remain above ground, and spring has begun. The Germans believe that if you make love when it rains, the resulting child will be a girl.

One of the most interesting dreams I had about nature happened when I worked as a volunteer on a kibbutz in Israel. I dreamed there was an earthquake that flattened the city of Haifa. As we strolled through the banana plantations, I began to recount my dream to my friend. As I finished speaking, the earth below us shook vigorously for a few moments. The *Jerusalem Post* said that the epicenter of the tremor was Haifa. Fortunately, my dream had exaggerated the event, and there was little damage. However, this is an interesting example of how close to nature we can be during dreams.

Superstition says that dreams about fine weather predict happy events, and unpleasant weather foretells troubles ahead. The psychological meaning of weather in a dream may indicate your state of mind. Stormy skies may show emotional troubles; sunny skies, happiness; rain may show release from tension; and snow may indicate that your emotions are frozen.

SIGNS, STORIES, EXPERIMENTS, AND SYMBOLS

A fun experiment to try is to keep records of your dreams and to highlight any that feature the weather. Weathermen can forecast the short-term weather with accuracy, but they have a lot of trouble predicting the long term. With the advent of global warming, we are likely to have a lot of "interesting" weather in the future, so dream insight into upcoming climate, forest fires, eruptions, and droughts may prove useful.

Try some of the dream incubation techniques described in this book to ask your dreams, "What will the weather be like in a month's time?" If you dream on January 1st of a rainy day, make a note that February 2nd will be rainy, and so on. Eventually, you may be able to plot the weather. Get this right and you can try the same technique to predict the stock market.

The table on the next page shows some of the traditional dream meanings associated with the **weather**. Some superstitions need to be taken with a grain of salt. See the **Symbolism** entry for advice about the psychological way to interpret dream meanings.

See also: **Dream Incubation (Seeding)**

Good Omens		Bad Omens	
Air	A clear blue sky brings success in your enterprises, successful lawsuits, safe journeys, and happiness in love.	Altitude	If you are perilously high in the air, you will make wrong decisions.
Clouds over the sun	Someone may try to prevent a partnership.	Barometer	Changes lie ahead. If it is broken, the changes will be for the worse.
Fall (Autumn)	Domestic happiness and a legacy lie ahead.	Cirrus clouds	You'll have difficulties in the future, but you will eventually succeed.
Forecast	Trust your own judgment.	Dark clouds	A sign of illness and business disappointments.
Gloom	A gloomy sky requires that you persevere.	Frost	You are acting like a fool.
Heaven	To ascend to heaven predicts authority and power.	Hail	Beware of the envy of others.
Ice	You will experience success after adversity.	Mirage	To dream of a desert mirage means you will lose friends.
Lightning	This indicates sudden success.	Mist	This is a bad omen for traders.
Rainbow	Your troubles are ending. In the east, healing. In the west, this is a good omen if you are already rich. Rainbows can also foretell good news, travel, and marriage.	Obscured sun	When the sun is completely obscured or disappears, this is a very bad sign for everyone except criminals.
Red sky	You will fall in love but fail in business.	Rain	You are warned of problems, troubles, and losses.
Shower	You will find success in your present undertakings.	Summer	This is only a good omen if you dream of summer during winter. All other times are bad omens.
Sudden shower	This indicates good luck in love and prosperity.	Sundial	There will be a death and a marriage.
Sun	Success and happiness lie ahead. Sunrise and sunset indicate beneficial changes.	Thermometer	People will mock you for your poor dress sense.
Tempest	To dream you are in a tempest means you will become very rich.	Thick clouds	Arguments are brewing.
Thunder	This is a good omen of success in all things. For farmers, it means abundant crops.	Thunderbolt	You will be forced to move.
White clouds	These are an indication of prosperity.	Tornado	Watch out, Dorothy. This dream means trouble at home.
Winter	This foretells of prosperity.	Wind	You will fight and win many battles throughout your life.

NUMEROLOGY

Nature's great book is written in mathematical symbols.

GALILEO, ITALIAN ASTRONOMER AND PHYSICIST

Numbers have always been associated with good luck or bad luck. They can also tell us a great deal about our destiny. Some numbers have had good or bad associations for centuries. Numerologists, who study the mystical significance of numbers, believe that numbers reveal a great deal about your fortune and personality and can provide insight into the auspiciousness of a dream.

Today, there is a growing interest in using numerology to unlock the mystical meaning of dreams. Numbers and dates that occur in dreams may be analyzed to determine if they predict good fortune or problems. You can do the same with names that appear in dreams because the letters can be converted to numbers and added together. You can examine the resulting number to determine whether or not the dream was fortuitous.

SIGNS, STORIES, EXPERIMENTS, AND SYMBOLS

Numerology is also used in conjunction with the Tarot or Runes to interpret dreams. Every Tarot card has a numerological meaning and an associated element—earth, air, fire, or water. These elements may be identified in a dream. When examined with their numerological meaning, they may help to identify the meaning of the dream. The elements are also associated with the astrological sun signs, so dreams featuring elements may be talking about people with these signs.

The following chart shows the elements together with their associated numbers and dream theme meanings.

Earth	4, 8	Practicality, honesty, success, fear	Taurus, Virgo, and Capricorn
Air	1, 5	Thoughts, plans, spirituality	Gemini, Libra, and Aquarius
Fire	3, 9	New ideas, passion, romance	Aries, Leo, and Sagittarius
Water	2, 6, 7	Emotions and strategy	Cancer, Scorpio, and Pisces

The main numerology system we use today assigns meanings to the numbers 1 to 9, which have mystical significance if seen in a dream. Other numbers may be added together to form just one number. For example, if you dream of the number 5378, you add the digits together: 5+3+7+8=23 Then, add them again: 2+3=5. The vibration of the number in the dream is 5, which can be interpreted.

I have also included the letters associated with each number. You can replace the letters with numbers, add them together, and reduce them to get one number. For example, if you dream of a windmill, you can discover the numerological significance:

(W) 5+(I) 9+(N) 5+(D) 4+(M) 4+(I) 9+(L) 3+(L) 3=42

4+2=6

6 = Peace and harmony in your life.

The chart at the top of page 67 shows the traditional numerical meanings.

Dreaming of numbers may give clues to your destiny.

TRADITIONAL NUMERICAL MEANINGS
1=A J S—Source of energy, initiation, creativity.
2=B K T—Beauty, culture, truth, honesty.
3=C LU—Enlightenment, trinity, communication, exaggeration, luck.
4=D M V—Security, stability, home, building, stubbornness.
5=E N W—Uncertainty, doubt, changeability, humor, quick thinking.
6=F O X—Peace, harmony, arts, reclusiveness, obstinacy, friendship, romance.
7=G P Y—Spirituality, wisdom, philosophy, empathy, meditation, intuition.
8=H Q Z—Justice, strength, money, will power, hard work.
9=I R—Dominance, psychic, freedom, reform, quarrels, human rights, destiny.

NUMINOUS DREAMS (GRAND DREAMS)

Peace can be reached through meditation on the knowledge which dreams give. Peace can also be reached through concentration upon that which is dearest to the heart.

PATANJALI, INDIAN AUTHOR

Most of the world's religions believe that although dreams are usually about everyday things, there are some special dreams that reveal the divine and can bring people into direct contact with God. Occasionally, everyone has a dream with a heaven-sent meaning. These dreams have a special energy and vividness, and they may have a profound and long-term effect on the dreamer.

Carl Jung referred to these momentous experiences as "numinous dreams," or often simply as "big dreams." The term "numinous"
was coined by Rudolf Otto to describe a force that involuntarily controls a person. Inexplicable mystical and holy experiences can be described as numinous. Jung said that if people could appreciate these dreams, their meaning would become "the richest jewels in the treasure-house of the soul."

Numinous dreams can have a transforming effect. They may relate directly to your personal life and connect you to the universal hopes and fears of humankind. These dreams expand your consciousness and give you insight into extended experience and meaning. Numinous dreams have a special quality and a feeling that Jung described as being spiritually elevated and touching the divine.

Psychic dreams arise via the collective unconscious described by Jung and are sometimes tainted with its mythical archetypal symbolism. You can recognize a psychic dream because it will often contain information that has no correspondence with the "day residue" of your personal unconscious. These dreams have a feeling about them as if they have come from the outside, from the unconscious or perhaps from outside of yourself.

Could it be that when you dream you may sometimes connect to what mystics call the Universal Mind? In my other books, I have argued that all life is connected together like a huge mycelium of life energy. This may even happen at the quantum level of reality where here and there, past and present become as one. Jung hinted at this idea when he spoke about the "Unus Mundus." He defined this as the unity of all things outside human categories, beyond our separation of reality into physical and mental states. Psychic dreams may occur when you connect with that part of your being that is at one with this universal mind. (See **Universal Mind.**)

Numinous dreams may occur when you have encountered something of great spiritual significance. You may have personally changed in some way by integrating hitherto unconscious parts of your personality. Jung noticed that when these important inner transformations take place, they are sometimes accompanied by odd occurrences in the external world, such as strange coincidences that correspond in some way with these numinous dreams.

My Internet spiritual community is very important to me. It has become an important part of my spiritual work and of the work of other spiritual helpers, many of whom are homebound due to illness. As our important work progressed, Vi Kipling, one of my most important disabled helpers and a retired spiritualist, had a numinous dream that inspired us forward. Her dream is a good example of a numinous dream. I believe the meaning of the dream is self-evident.

Vi wrote, "Last night, I had what I tend to call one of my significant dreams. These dreams are always meaningful, and I recognize them for what they are. Upon waking, I can remember every single detail, which I would like to share with you. The feeling that came with the dream was that it did not involve just me.

"I was given a day-old **baby** girl. She was so beautiful, with that soft, downy, peachy colored skin so velvety to the touch and with big, unfocused blue eyes. I held her tightly and stroked her cheek, and she chuckled. I couldn't believe it. I called to Bill (hubby) to come and say hello, so he came to look at her and, feeling stupid like men do, held her hand and said, 'Hello, little one,' and she gurgled right on cue.

"We sat and all watched TV in the evening, and this baby was laughing at the jokes even before I got them. She responded to us when we spoke, but not with words, with gurgles and the little baby noises they make. I couldn't fathom what was happening, as this baby was one day old.

"The only way to describe her is 'she was incredibly beautiful, perfection personified.' I never try to interpret dreams, but I knew exactly what this meant. I have been given, or am part of, something new which is going to develop so quickly and which is incredibly beautiful. When I awoke, I still retained a feeling of awe, for want of a better word."

OMENS

The waking have one world in common;
sleepers have each a private world of their own.

HERACLITUS, GREEK PHILOSOPHER

Superstition tells us that you must never tell a dream before breakfast and never relate a dream that occurs on Friday if it is bad. The proverb says, "**Friday**'s dream on **Saturday** told, is sure to come true before nine days old."

For most people, omens are only antiquated superstitions, yet a surprising number of people secretly believe in them. Many of the dream dictionaries on the market today, and particularly those that deal with dreams about the future, rely on superstition and ignore the discoveries of psychology. The unconscious speaks in symbolism, metaphor, and allegory. Therefore, a long list of dream meanings based only on superstitions is not particularly helpful when trying to unravel the real meaning of a dream. According to Aristotle, "The skillful interpreter of dreams is he who has the faculty of observing resemblances." This is the ability you need to develop if you wish to understand the hidden meaning of your dreams or to know their prophetic value.

Certainly many people are credulous, and omens and superstitions can cater to the insecurities and weakness in human nature. However, could it be that there are factors that influence our lives that are not governed by the laws of causality? The psychologist Carl Jung spoke about how psychological and actual events will synchronize. I mentioned elsewhere in this book (page 30) that a beetle flew into Jung's consultation room as his patient spoke about a scarab beetle. I, too, have witnessed many remarkable coincidences that have proven to me that not everything in life follows an orderly pattern.

The earliest records of omens and dreams are from the time of the Babylonian and Assyrian civilizations. The priests of these times would deduce omens from the appearance and actions of mammals, birds, fish, and reptiles. Signs were also observed from the condition of human or mammal offspring, or from the symptoms of sick people. Omens would be seen in the appearance of a man's shadow, from the images seen in fire or smoke, and in the forms seen in the landscape. My personal favorite, and one not to be tried in the living room, is to look for signs and omens in the entrails of sacrificial victims.

Most of the superstitions today about dreams have very ancient origins, going back to the time when omens influenced people's lives.

SIGNS, STORIES, EXPERIMENTS, AND SYMBOLS

Omens occur in daily life and during sleep, and it is believed that to disobey an omen is to court trouble. However, there are no fixed laws as to the truth of omens. Superstitious people will believe that trouble is approaching if they see or dream about a bad omen, but any fullfilment of the omen is probably more the result of coincidence than of fate. And of course, attitude is important, too. When Julius Caesar landed at Adrumetum in Africa, he slipped and fell. This was considered a terrible omen, but the quick-thinking Caesar exclaimed, "Thus, do I take possession of thee, O Africa."

See also: **Oneiromancy, Superstition**

ONEIROMANCY

When the human race has once acquired a superstition, nothing short of death is ever likely to remove it.

MARK TWAIN, AUTHOR

Writings about dreams date back to the earliest times. In many ancient cultures, dreams were seen as portents of the gods. The Egyptian priests of the falcon-headed god Horus compiled one of the earliest dream documents. This papyrus dates from approximately 1250 B.C. and records over 200 dreams and their prophetic meanings. The art of divination by dreams is called oneiromancy and has been practiced everywhere in the world throughout history.

In the second century A.D., Artemidorus of Ephesus wrote the oldest surviving book about interpreting dreams. While traveling extensively, he researched and wrote his book, interviewing people about their dreams and the outcome of the dreams. He may be the father of oneiromancy because he was primarily interested in discovering whether dreams could tell the future.

Freud took an interest in the book, and I wonder what he made of this dream cited in Artemidorus's *Interpretation of Dreams* (5:91): "A man dreamt that he had three **penises**. He was a slave at the time and was set free. He then had three names instead of one, since he acquired an additional two names from the man who had set him free."

Artemidorus also points out that sometimes a dream can have different meanings for different people. He cites examples of pregnant women dreaming about **snakes**. For example, a woman dreamed of giving birth to a snake, and her son grew to become a great public speaker. Says Artemidorus, "For

a serpent has a forked tongue, which is also true of a public speaker."

But six other women he met had the same dream, and the destinies of their children were different. One became a hiero-phant (priest), and in this instance "the **serpent** is a sacred animal and plays a part in secret rites." Another's son became a prophet, "for the serpent is sacred to Apollo who is the most versed in prophecy." A fourth woman's child "turned out to be undisciplined and wanton, and he committed adultery with many of the women in the city. For the serpent slips through the most narrow holes and attempts to escape detection by observers." Another's child "was apprehended in a robbery and was beheaded. For whenever a serpent is caught, it is struck over the head and dies in this way." A sixth woman had the same dream, and her child became a runaway slave. "For the serpent does not follow a straight path." Yet another woman had the same dream, and her child became a paralytic. "For the serpent must employ its entire body to travel anywhere, which is also true of para-lytics."

It is interesting that Artemidorus makes the point that there are many ways to inter-pret prophetic dream images, yet his work became the main influence for the dream dictionaries that are still in use today. These insist on nailing down specific meanings for specific dreams. Clearly flexibility of inter-pretation is important.

SIGNS, STORIES, EXPERIMENTS, AND SYMBOLS

Oneiromancy classifies prophetic dream images into the following categories:

Sharp Objects: Swords, knives, scissors, and so on tell of bad news to come.

Ascending: Going up a **ladder**, **rope**, **stair**, or **escalator** is a sign of good fortune.

Descending: Going **downhill**, **falling**, or descending a **ladder**, etc. is a sign of reverses or failures.

Entertainment: Dreams of being entertained can represent either good or bad fortune. If you enjoy watching **television**, a **concert**, **film**, or **play**, then these are indications that happiness lies ahead in your life. But if the entertainment was dull, canceled, or not very good, there are problems afoot.

Abundance and Want: Many dreams contain symbols of **wealth** or austerity. For example, a full **wallet** is an auspicious oracle and can indicate forthcoming wealth; the reverse is true if the wallet is empty. Similarly, a calm **sea** or fine **weather** shows easy progress, but rough **water** or stormy skies indicate ill luck. Some images that can mean either good or bad luck include **air**, **banks**, **barns**, **bowls**, **buckets**, **cages**, **canals**, **cellars**, **clouds**, **cups**, **drinks**, **farms**, **fields**, **gardens**, **glass**, **harvests**, **landscapes**, **letters**, **markets**, **paths**, **plants**, **smells**, **streets**, and **wind**.

Obstacles: Based on traditional oneiromancy, obstacle symbols are important in the dream dictionaries. An obstacle may have many degrees of misfortune predicted. For example, a **door** that opens easily is considered a sign of only minor difficulties. However, if it is **locked** or jammed, then insurmountable problems lie ahead. Symbols that are traditionally interpreted as obstacle dreams include **abysses**, **bolts**, **canyons**, **caves**, **cliffs**, **crutches**, **ditches**, **examinations**, **fences**, **floods**, **gates**, **handcuffs**, **hedges**, **hills**, **labyrinths**, **locks**, **mountains**, prisons, **questions**, **rivalry**, **rocks**, **struggling**, **towers**, **traffic** jams, **valleys**, **walls**, and **zoos**.

Contrary: As well as the examples above, some dreams are believed to predict the opposite of what happens in the dream. For example, if you dream of having an argument, this can mean that you are going to share affection with someone. Conversely, if you dream of giving affection to someone, it will mean that an argument is brewing. Could it be that some of the ancient oneiromancers were hedging their bets to cover dreams that didn't conform to their categories? Some other common dreams that are contrary include **ambition/setbacks**, **celebration/regrets**, **criticism/appreciation**, **crying/happiness**, **fear/courage**, **inferiority/superiority**, **loss/gain**, **peace/trouble**, **wealth/poverty**. Interestingly, the Chinese believe in reversing dream meanings. For them, too, **crying** is a dream symbol of happiness, and if a group of people are seen crying together, this will drive away malevolent **ghosts**.

See also: **Omens, Tribal Dream Interpretation**

ORACLES

For more than thirty years, I have interested myself in this oracle technique, or method of exploring the unconscious, for it has seemed to me of uncommon significance.

CARL JUNG, SWISS PSYCHOLOGIST

Many of the oracles used by psychics are full of what Carl Jung referred to as "archetypal symbols." An archetype is what Freud called "archaic remnants" and what Jung thought of as "primordial images."

Jungian psychology believes that these universal symbols are passed from generation to generation like biological traits. They are found in myths and religions the world over. In particular, the Tarot cards deal with archetypal symbols of the human situation as reflected in our own lives. These help us better understand ourselves. They are the symbols that appear and reappear in our dreams.

Carl Jung wrote and gave many lectures about the use of oracles and meaningful chance. He was interested in the psychological aspects of time, number, and methods of divining fate, such as the *I Ching*, astrology, Tarot, runes, palmistry, and dice.

In particular, Jung was interested in the imagery used in these oracles and in how this imagery corresponds to many of the symbols found in dreams. Oracles, and especially the major arcana, or trump cards, of the Tarot, have been used effectively in therapy. Tarot symbols, for example, can be used to stimulate the imagination of the client.

The Tarot cards contain many of the archetypal symbols of Jungian psychology, including the shadow, the anima and animus, and the wise old man. There are also many symbols that represent archetypes of the transformative processes such as the hero, the sacrifice, rebirth, the mother, and the self.

SIGNS, STORIES, EXPERIMENTS, AND SYMBOLS

If you have an interest in Tarot cards or are learning to read them, your dreams may make specific references to cards. These symbols may reveal information about yourself and, in some instances, may be prophecies for the future. Even if you have no knowledge of the Tarot, related imagery may spontaneously appear in your dreams. These images may be interpreted in a way that is similar to the cards and may have similar forecasts for the future.

Included below are the Jungian dream meanings for the 22 major arcana cards from the 78 Tarot deck together with their traditional fortune-telling meanings.

The Fool: This is Jung's archetype of the divine child, such as the infant **Christ**. It may show the birth of a **hero**. In a psychological sense, it is the beginning of the inner journey to spirituality; it is the archetypal wanderer.

Forecast: A journey, the novice, innocence as a protector.

The Magician: This is the divine messenger, Mercury, Hermes, and Thoth. This symbol represents the power of free will to bring about transformation. Because of associations with sleight of hand, it may to a lesser extent suggest the archetype of the trickster (the animal aspect of ourselves that is unreasoning).

Forecast: Self-control, skill, taking charge.

The High Priestess: This symbol is associated with the goddess Isis or Artemis, the huntress. The card represents the intuition, and the imagery may represent the unconscious. In particular, it may represent the **anima**, the female aspect of the mind. Jungian psychologists have linked it to the archetype of the **virgin**.

Forecast: Intuition, wisdom, mysteries, secrets, tenacity.

The Empress: This card represents nature and the feminine side of the psyche. The symbolism suggests Jung's archetype of the **mother** and feminine authority. In a dream, she may show your feminine tendencies.

Forecast: Fertility, abundance, mother, health, kindliness.

The Emperor: This image represents the masculine side of the psyche or any strong masculine authority. It is closely associated with Jung's archetype of the **father** as well as the **hero**. In your dream, he may show your masculine tendencies.

Forecast: Willpower, ambition, stability, father, benefactor.

The Hierophant: This image may represent the spiritual conscience. It is a religious figure and may suggest the Jungian archetype of the religious teacher. Some Jungian psychologists say it is the archetype of the **wise old man**.

Forecast: Marriage, good advice, religion, the higher self, mercy.

The Lovers: This symbol suggests the union of opposites, especially masculinity and femininity, **anima** and **animus**. Jung believed that our spiritual goal is to bring these opposites within the psyche into harmony. In dreams, lovers are sometimes the other side of ourselves.

Forecast: Love, sexual union, beauty, emotional success, trials overcome.

The Chariot: This card represents Jung's "persona," the self we show to the world. The imagery also suggests the archetype of the warrior, the hero who seeks out the truth. It is full of drive toward a fixed goal and thus a victory. It also suggests the spiritual impulse that sooner or later will drive you to seek to discover your true nature.

Forecast: The driving force, triumph, war, vengeance, providence.

Justice: The symbolism represents the law of karma (cause and effect). As with the Hierophant, this card can also represent the conscience with relation to material affairs and self-judgment. In a dream, it may show the part of you that is moral.

Forecast: The law, truth, balance, control, a contract.

The Hermit: The theme of this image is the wise old sage. He is the inner guiding light of the higher self. The lamp he carries may show the powers of the intuition. This symbol represents withdrawal and meditation. It is reminiscent of Jung's archetype of the wise old man.

Forecast: Prudence, a lonely spiritual quest, treason, caution, inertia.

The Wheel of Fortune: The wheel symbolizes the law of cyclic manifestation. It may also hint at past lives and the cycle of reincarnation. Similar imagery in a psychic dream may represent psychological growth and suggest the archetypes of fate and destiny.

Forecast: The hand of fate, a turn for the better, luck, destiny, abundance.

Strength: Most decks use the symbol of the lion for this card. Sometimes, a woman controls the beast. The card shows controlled strength, courage, and inner resolve. The dream symbolism suggests the archetypes of goodness and endurance.

Forecast: Fortitude, courage, energy, success, self-discipline.

The Hanged Man: This card stands for selfless sacrifice for the purpose of helping

The dreaming mind can use symbols of well-known oracles to express hidden meanings.

others. The imagery of the card indicates the archetypes of sacrifice and initiation. It also is suggestive of the archetype of dying gods, such as Jesus. The symbolism in a dream may be a prelude to spiritual rebirth and the ending of a difficult period in your life.

Forecast: Wisdom in difficulties, **self-sacrifice**, intuition, initiation, prophecy.

Death: This card shows the ending of a cycle so a new one can begin. Death also suggests change and spiritual transformation. This card indicates sudden change and, in a dream, may show that you are experiencing many psychological changes. The imagery relates to Jung's archetype of rebirth.

Forecast: Transformation, events beyond your control, inevitable changes.

Temperance: This card shows the skill that is required to persevere. It also illustrates how to make the best of difficult situations. The card shows communication between heaven and earth; psychologically, it may represent the union of opposites as from Jungian psychology.

Forecast: Management, economy, transcendence, wise counsel.

The Devil: This dark card represents slavery or confinement and, in particular, bondage to the desires. The imagery also indicates the harm caused by an inflated ego. From a Freudian standpoint, the card shows the libido, psychological and sexual energy. In a dream, it may represent an animalistic aspect of sexuality.

Forecast: Anger, **violence**, jealousy, greed, deceit, instinct, sexual passion.

The Tower: The card shows a stone tower destroyed by lightning. It is a symbol for unexpected bad luck and ruin. In a dream, a destroyed tower may show despair and breakdown. It may also indicate sexual worries, because the tower is a phallic symbol. This card represents catastrophe. The imagery of the card suggests the archetype of chaos.

Forecast: Catastrophe, repossession, ruin, adversity, calamity.

The Star: This is a card of hope and promise. Just as a star may guide a ship, so hope may guide your life. Some Jungian psychologists say that the star symbolizes that part of the personality that survives death. It is the spiritual part of the psyche.

Forecast: Hope, goals, expectations, guiding force, enlightenment, bright prospects.

The Moon: The moon represents the instincts and is a symbol for the female aspect of the self, the anima. It is closely associated with the intuition and the instincts. In the Tarot, the card also shows irrational fears.

Forecast: Dark forces, nightmares, illusion, hidden fears, danger overcome through intuition.

The Sun: As the giver of light, the sun represents life and the forces of conscious creativity. The imagery of this card suggests growth, success, and abundance. The sun is an archetype of God and full consciousness.

Forecast: **Happiness**, joy, freedom, happy marriage, success, health, fertility.

The Judgment: The symbolism of this card suggests the archetypes of evaluation, reward, and completion. Some versions show people rising from the grave, a symbol of spiritual rebirth and release from ignorance and bondage.

Forecast: A major decision, outcome, final result, **rebirth**, problems overcome.

The World: The card indicates completion. The imagery of this card is a circle indicating the archetypes of wholeness, synthesis, and perfection. The circle is the perfect **mandala**, the archetypal symbol that appears in dreams, representing spiritual perfection and wholeness.

Forecast: Successful completion, assured success, recognition, long-distance travel, harmony.

ORIENTAL DREAMS

Man is a genius when he is dreaming.

AKIRA KUROSAWA,
JAPANESE FILMMAKER

The Chinese are among the most superstitious people in the world. Their dream symbols are packed with luck themes. In China, one of the most auspicious symbols is the phoenix. If a phoenix speaks in a dream, it is always said to predict the future. The Chinese phoenix has brightly colored feathers. Some say that these quills indicate that the dreamer will become a great writer. (I have not had that dream yet!) Another Chinese omen of literary talent is to dream of cutting out the heart.

The Japanese emperors sought political guidance in their dreams. The royal palace in Kyushu once contained an incubation bed, made of polished stone, for inducing dreams. Shrines for incubating dreams still exist in many Shinto temples, the most famous being the temple at Usa on the southern island of Kyushu. Dreams are sought as visions to help answer questions that are plaguing the waking self. Usually, the answers come from ancestral spirits.

The Japanese also believe that certain symbols have the same meaning to many different people. For example, a dream about **teeth** falling out is considered to be a sign of money coming to you. Modern interpretations of this dream state that this is a symbol for insecurity that often comes at a time of transition. It expresses feelings similar to the insecurity children feel when their milk teeth fall out as they approach maturity.

The Hindu religious text *Artharva-Veda* (c. 1000 B.C.) explains that the time a prophetic dream occurs will indicate when the event will take place. In other words, the dreams are prophetic, and the timing of the dream indicates how soon the prophecy will come to pass. Dreams that occur near dawn will happen sooner than those that are foretold in an early night dream. Dreams that are particularly vivid are believed to be influenced by the gods. Hindu philosophers spoke of them as "dreams under the influence of a deity."

Asian cultures are perhaps more open to the idea that dreams can be of benefit than are Western cultures. Perhaps the Western ego is more rigid and impervious and resists the unconscious as an enemy. Many Asian people have more permeable egos and, therefore, do not resist the power of the unconscious, greeting it as a friend instead.

Dreaming of a phoenix is very auspicious and can relate to future events.

Dreaming of a dragon implies good luck.

Some interesting Chinese dream symbols include hunting for **pigs**, which shows success and victory, and being **pregnant**, which augers great fortune and promotion to a position of high office. **Snakes** are indications of forthcoming evil, except yellow ones, which symbolize power. Dreams about **spiders** are also supposed to bring good luck because, like **turtles**, they are magical animals. Other Chinese good luck dreams include **dragons**, **stars**, clear **water**, **wells**, **silk**, **shaving**, **roosters**, **rain**, changing your **name**, and **tigers**. One of my personal Chinese favorites is dreaming of a bleeding **cow,** which for the Chinese is a portent for advancement and finding a higher position. I'm not going to tell you all the bad luck symbols for there are so many of them you'll never sleep. Nonetheless, here are a few inauspicious dreams: broken **vehicles**, **cats**, **cosmetics**, **doors**, white **dogs**, eating **pearls**, **singing**, and growing **horns**. Surprisingly, dreams about **coffins** are considered good for this is an omen of money to come. If you dream of entering a **tomb,** the ancestors will see to it that you become a rich person.

See also: **Dream Incubation (Seeding)**

OUT-OF-BODY EXPERIENCES (OBEs)

*Then the spirit lifted me up and I heard behind
me the noise of the Lord rumbling as the
glory of the Lord rose from its place.*

EZEKIEL 3:12

Out-of-body dreams, in which you "float" up and look down upon yourself or upon another location, are a form of psychic dream. Some psychics claim they visit other actual locations, often ones that they've never seen. Traveling out of the body is sometimes called astral projection.

Frederik van Eeden presented one of the first studies of out-of-body dreams to the Society of Psychical Research in 1913. Van Eeden had already presented evidence for lucid dreams in which the dreamer becomes conscious while the dream is taking place. He told the society that his own lucid dreams were often preceded for several nights by dreams of flying. Sometimes, these lucid dreams included information apparently received clairvoyantly that could be verified later. In other instances, he believed he left his body.

In one instance while "**flying**," he dreamed that he would be robbed of a large sum of money, an event that was to take place soon afterward. Of great interest to Van Eeden was that sometimes he would dream of lying on his stomach when in reality he was lying in bed on his back. If he allowed himself to awaken slowly, he would experience the sensation of slipping from his "dream body" that was lying face down, into his actual sleeping body.

Depending upon the person, the appearance of the "dream body" ranges from a gossamerlike form to an exact replica of the physical body. Having the ability to project consciousness can open up many interesting opportunities to the dreamer. Some people claim to be able to travel to remote locations. They claim to be able to walk the beaches of Hawaii, explore the ancient pyramids of Egypt, or even have a free ticket to the moon.

I have had many of these experiences myself. In most instances, however, I have found that it is hard to maintain consciousness for long periods of time. My own experience is one of projecting my awareness rather than a dream body. Nonetheless, on occasion I have looked down at my sleeping body from the ceiling and awakened with clear memories of having visited a remote location. Many people report having these experiences during puberty.

At first, the experience of being without a body is frightening if you have never heard about astral projection. It is natural to assume that you are dead and start to panic. The result is usually a quick return to the body. This rapid return is sometimes accompanied by sensations of a jolt to the physical body, a loud bang, and a flash of brilliant light. Once the initial fears are overcome, astral travel becomes natural and is not accompanied by any negative sensations.

SIGNS, STORIES, EXPERIMENTS, AND SYMBOLS

If you are able to dream lucidly or have super-real dreams, you may have the ability to project astrally. Some of the methods of astral projection include:

Lucid dream method: Laboratory studies have concluded that OBEs can occur in the same physiological state as lucid dreaming. Experience indicates that great enthusiasm to have an OBE will increase the likelihood of it happening, so read a lot about the subject and think about it before retiring. If you dream of flying or of being Superman, this is a prelude to astral projection. In the same way, you may dream of taking impossibly long steps or of being able to jump into the sky. Some experimenters use falling dreams as a means of launching the dream body. Once you are aware of flying in a dream, you can experiment with visiting other locations and dimensions.

Yoga method: Hatha yoga exercises are believed to increase the energy of the dream body and give the practitioner more control over the dream body's ability to separate from the physical body. A vegetarian/vegan diet is believed to aid in projection. Advanced techniques can be found in the Yoga Sutras and Tibetan Buddhist teachings.

Visionary method: Have you ever "seen" incredible visions in your mind's eye as you fall asleep? Images can seem to transform one into another in a fantastic flow of brilliantly colorful pictures. You may see incredible landscapes, strange faces, places, shapes, and patterns. Some people experience this as they fall asleep (hypnagogic dreaming), and a few experience this as they wake up (hypnopompic dreaming). Both of these states are used by psychics to trigger clairvoyance and astral travel. If you see a landscape in this state of consciousness, move toward it and try to hold this picture in your mind's eye. At first, you will experience remote viewing (seeing a distant place by clairvoyance), but in time you may be taken directly to the location in the dream body.

Relaxation method: Lying in bed in a dark room, put your body into a super-relaxed state. You can accomplish this by tightening and relaxing the muscles one by one from your feet to your face. Next, focus on letting your body become deeply relaxed and heavy, like clay. Look into the darkness through your closed eyelids. A point may come when you can "see" the room even though your eyes are closed. It may appear bathed in ultraviolet light. If you do not "see" the room, use your imagination to picture it. Focus on an object in the room, such as the ceiling light, and draw it toward you. This will help the dream body separate from the physical body. Sometimes, this is accompanied by a shaking sensation and a rumbling noise. Once you get close to the object, turn around to see your physical body lying in the bed.

See also: **Hypnagogic and Hypnopompic Dreaming, Lucid Dreams, Remote Viewing (RV)**

PARALYSIS

Frisbeetarianism is the philosophy that when you die, your soul goes up on a roof and gets stuck.

GEORGE CARLIN, COMEDIAN

Have you ever awakened from a dream to find your body completely paralyzed? You want to cry out, but the sound will not come out. You can open your eyes, but your body will not move. While in this frightening predicament, some people have also been aware that there is an evil presence in the room that may attack them.

What I have described is a condition psychologists call sleep paralysis. Recent surveys suggest that it affects between 25 and 30 percent of the population. People also frequently report feeling a "presence" that they describe as malevolent, threatening, or evil. An intense sense of dread and terror is very common. Sometimes, the "entity" may attack by strangling the sleeper, exerting crushing pressure on the chest. In some instances, the dreamer may believe that a malevolent spirit is raping him or her.

Fortunately, there are no paranormal forces involved; the condition is caused when the back of the brain comes to consciousness before the rest of the body "wakes up." This is more likely to happen if you are overly tired. Doctors also advise that it is best to sleep on your side and not on your back because this position can trigger the condition.

As we know from Freud, a great deal of dream content is of a sexual nature. It is conceivable that many of the sexual attacks people describe may simply be a vivid waking nightmare with a sexual undertone that occurs during a bout of sleep paralysis. Similarly, psychologists have explained that sleep paralysis may be at the root of cases in which people believe they have been abducted by aliens. Often such claims begin with a report of someone waking up terrified, feeling a presence, and being unable to move. The cases may include sexual "experiments" and often include waking dream-type hallucinations.

If you find yourself in the midst of a sleep-paralysis episode, you might try a traditional method for overcoming the paralysis by attempting to move your fingers, toes, or even your tongue. A number of people have suggested rapidly moving your eyes back and forth as a way of bringing a bout of SP to an end. As it is possible to have multiple episodes in a single night, it may help to get up briefly and move around after any such episode before trying to sleep again.

SIGNS, STORIES, EXPERIMENTS, AND SYMBOLS

Dreams about paralysis can also have a symbolic meaning. The dream may be saying that you are concerned about being trapped in a particular situation and that you want to escape. For example, you may feel dissatisfied

During sleep paralysis, the dreamer may become aware of a malevolent presence.

with a relationship or have an unsatisfying career. A dream in which someone else is paralyzed may represent an aspect of yourself that you are not expressing. Similarly, if you dream of a paralyzed animal, your dream may indicate that your instincts and sexual feelings are being inhibited.

According to superstition, you should reverse this dream and probably can expect an expansive period ahead. I do not subscribe to this belief about reversing meanings to understand a prophecy. Dreams can give specific insights or may distort things, but they do not cloak meanings in reverse symbolism. If your dream is not describing your feelings about your current situation, it may be anticipating potential problems on the horizon.

See also: **Out-of-Body Experiences (OBEs), Psychic Attacks**

PARAPSYCHOLOGY

On the periphery of sleep, I heard a voice telling me that I must get well and build an "edifice" that would honor the subject to which I had devoted my life. I awoke with a feeling of deep conviction that I must begin to build a new structure containing the best elements of my own work.

EILEEN J. GARRETT, PARAPSYCHOLOGIST

Parapsychology is a term coined by J.B. Rhine to refer to the experimental and quantitative study of paranormal phenomena. Currently, it is generally used instead of "psychical research" to refer to all scientific investigation of the paranormal. Much of this research has centered around the apparent ESP that occurs during dreams.

Sigmund Freud, considered the father of modern psychiatry, proposed that dreams serve as windows into the psyche and reveal unfulfilled wishes and desires expressed through symbolism. He also believed that sometimes ESP occurs in dreams. In 1925, Sigmund Freud created a scandal by writing in a memorandum to the members of his inner circle that he believed in mental telepathy and that he had undertaken tests that convinced him of the existence of such phenomena. Freud retracted and stated that, "...my adherence to telepathy is my private affair like my Jewishness, my passion for smoking, and other things, and the theme of telepathy—inessential for psychoanalysis." Nonetheless, Freud was so impressed by Cecil Murray's report on telepathic experiments at the Society for Psychical Research that he was "prepared to give up my resistances to the existence of thought transference."

The pioneering psychologist Carl Jung proposed a theory of spiritual archetypes that he believed occurred in dreams which came from the collective unconscious. In his autobiography, Jung cites many instances of psychic dreams that clearly show they were a recurrent influence in his life and work. The scientific community's resistance was such that he only dared write about them openly toward the end of his life.

Many scientists have viewed parapsychology with great suspicion because the term has come to be associated with a variety of supernatural phenomena and pseudoscience. Parapsychologists study "anomalous" phenomena. These are things that are difficult to explain within current scientific models. Generally, this includes Extra Sensory Perception (ESP), Psychokinesis (PK), and phenomena suggestive of survival after bodily death, including out-of-body experiences (OBEs), near-death experiences (NDEs), apparitions, and reincarnation. Many of these themes may be experienced in dreams.

Important work in the field of psychic dreaming and altered states of consciousness during sleep has been done by the parapsychologists Ullman, Krippner, and Vaughan. They conducted elaborate dream telepathy experiments during the 1970s. If you are interested in the scientific basis of psychic dreaming, their work is worth detailed study. I have already spoken about the pioneering work of Joseph Banks Rhine in the ESP section, but others worthy of further reading include Eileen J. Garrett, Charles C. Tart, Celia Green, Fred Alan Wolfe, and Robert Moss.

Some psychologists today believe that dreams are nothing more than the mind's way of allowing the emotions to calm down. Without dreams, we would simply overheat. Dreams may be unnecessary bits of information being cleared from your memory, just as a computer's files are cleaned of unwanted data. Conversely, the ancients regarded sleep as a second life during which the soul was freed from the body and had access to the past and future. The tide of scientific materialism is turning, and today many researchers believe that dreams can have paranormal content. Like their ancient forefathers, they believe dreams may have a psychic element that reveals information about the past, present, and future.

SIGNS, STORIES, EXPERIMENTS, AND SYMBOLS

Carl Jung had many paranormal visions in dreams, and he recalled many of these in his autobiography, *Memories, Dreams, Reflections*. Some of his most interesting dream visions happened toward the end of his life, as he approached death. In one vivid dream, he saw the "other Bollingen," his home beside the upper lake of Zürich, bathed in a glow of light. A voice told him that it was completed and ready for habitation. The golden tower on the other shore of the lake "was now ready for him to move into." Jung died in Küsnacht, near Zürich, at a 3:45 p.m. on Tuesday afternoon, June 6, 1961. An hour later, lightning struck a tall popular tree in his garden at the lake's edge.

See also: **Extra Sensory Perception (ESP)**

PAST LIVES

If Lincoln was alive today, he'd roll over in his grave.

GERALD FORD, FORMER PRESIDENT OF THE UNITED STATES

Have you ever dreamed of other times and other places where you played the part of characters completely removed from your normal experience? Perhaps you have awakened with a powerful sense of déjà vu and known that the unfamiliar surroundings of your dream are revealing memories from long ago. And perhaps this same eerie feeling sometimes persists into waking life with certain ancient places stimulating feelings similar to the ones you felt in your dreams.

People who believe in reincarnation argue that dreams can bring an awareness of memories from previous incarnations. These dreams of past lives have certain qualities about them that differentiate them from ordinary dreams. The dreams are set in the past, of course, but they are also accompanied by a strong sense of familiarity.

Past-life dreams tend to recur, but they do not have exactly the same content every time. Each dream may show different aspects of your previous life. For example, I dream of an ancient farm setting that I believe may be the echoes of a memory from a past life. Yet every time I return to the dream, it is slightly different, and a new "memory" about the place is retrieved. From this series of dreams that have happened over 30 years, I have been able to draw a comparatively detailed map, which I hope one day to be able to match to a real historic place.

In past-life dreams, you usually participate in what is happening. Sometimes, you may see yourself from a different perspective, such as seeing yourself dressed in Roman clothing, but in most instances there is a sense of taking part in and a familiarity with what you do. You see things from the perspective of the "you" from your former life.

Past-life dreams may also show you at various ages during your former incarnation and may highlight familiar routines as well as dramatic events. A life as a knight, for example, may show your apprenticeship, advancement, marriage, battles, and even your death. It will probably also include the mundane, such as mealtimes, as well as the excitement of battle. All of this will be revealed in short and perhaps initially unrelated glimpses until the story of this incarnation is eventually revealed. The dream revelations may start during childhood and unfold in dreams throughout your life.

In many instances, you will not recognize some of the dreams that belong to the sequence, so keep a detailed dream diary to fully assimilate the information you are being given. Keeping careful records may also reveal not just one but many past-life memories. An insight into the problems and joys you had in former incarnations will help you identify some of the fears and doubts that may inhibit you in this life.

Clearly, it is not good to live in the past, but these memories may be useful. They may help you identify and deal with the hidden factors running in the background of your awareness. For example, you may identify destructive behavior patterns in relationships and see how past-life experiences have locked you into a particular pattern of behavior. By understanding these past-life dreams, you will be empowered to change the negative influences into something positive. For instance, if you were bullied in a past life, this may undermine your confidence in this life. Thus, you may seek out abusive partners or enter relationships that you know will fail. Retrieving this memory brings these traits to light and disempowers them. There is the realization that the people from your former life can no longer harm you. As a result, you may now move toward greater confidence and happiness in this life. Knowledge of the past frees you from its hidden chains.

SIGNS, STORIES, EXPERIMENTS, AND SYMBOLS

At the battlefield in Langres, France, General George Patton told his driver that he already knew the place. He told his driver where to go and said it was as if someone were whispering directions in his ear. He correctly went to the ancient Roman Amphitheater, the Drill Grounds, the Forum, and even correctly went to the spot where Caesar had pitched his tent. "You see, I've been here before," he said.

PEOPLE

I don't design clothes; I design dreams.

RALPH LAUREN, FASHION DESIGNER

Jungian psychologists believe the people in our dreams are not our mothers, sisters, friends, or movie stars but are symbols representing aspects of our own psyche. Often they represent abstract things that are too hard to express any other way. Another person appearing in your dream may represent aspects of your own character. For example, a person who is known to be short-tempered may represent your own angry attitude; your mother or a motherly person may represent your qualities of kindness; and someone you

remember who has stolen things in the past may represent your secrets.

In most instances, the people in your dreams are symbols of yourself. Of course, there will also be times when your dreams may represent the actual person. Don't frighten yourself by believing that something terrible is going to happen to them just because you dreamed it would. First, ask yourself about the symbolic meaning of the dream before assuming that a dream is an omen. For example, if you dream of a loved one dying, ask yourself what this person may represent about your own nature. Perhaps the side of yourself that this person represents is not being expressed in your everyday life.

Good Omens		Bad Omens	
Alien	You will make new friends (possibly green ones).	*Acrobat*	Beware of accidents and particularly those connected with travel.
Bride	To dream of seeing a bride is generally fortunate, but some say it means a love or business rival.	*Baby*	An ugly baby means treacherous friends, but an attractive one means good friends.
Cannibalism	A wonderful dream that indicates enrichment unless the body is that of a hanged man.	*Bridegroom*	This indicates unexpected delays but good luck with legal affairs.
Doll	Domestic happiness lies ahead.	*Gondolier*	Your romantic life will be dull and boring.
Juggler	You will make money easily.	*Gypsy*	This foretells problems with travel arrangements.
Knight	You will be protected from harm.	*Judge*	There will be setbacks.
Messenger	Look out for a lucrative offer.	*Lawyer*	Business worries are likely.
Parents	This indicates happiness and achievements.	*Teacher*	You will be invited to a solemn occasion.
Strangers	A happy reunion is prophesied.	*Visitor*	If you are the visitor, this shows your friends are false. It can also mean a birth.
Wizard	This predicts prosperity for the whole family.	*Waiter*	You will nurse an invalid.
Zulu	This indicates release from danger or health worries.	*Widower*	Your partner will desert you. For single people, your date will deceive you.

The table on the previous page shows some of the traditional dream meanings associated with people. Some superstitions need to be taken with a grain of salt. See the **Symbolism** entry for advice about the psychological way to interpret dream meanings.

PRECOGNITION

Time is an illusion perpetrated by the manufacturers of space.

GRAFFITO

Precognition is the paranormal awareness of future events. Foreseeing the future in a dream is an example of precognition. This may include prophecies and predictions that claim to foretell future events. Premonitions, or intuitive experiences, are also believed to foretell future events.

For instance, I dreamed about learning to fly an airplane at a flying school in Florida. With me were a number of Arabic students. I assumed the dream had something to do with my past at a London flying school (which has a branch in Florida). The school had been one of my clients when I worked as a graphic designer. A few days later, when two airplanes hit the World Trade Center, I did not connect the dream with the event. However, further news coverage revealed that the terrorists had only recently attended a flying school in order to learn enough to steer a plane into a building. This dream is an example of precognition.

President Lincoln had a more famous dream precognition than I did. Two weeks before his assassination, he dreamed that there was a funeral at the White House. In the dream, he asked a soldier who was in the casket, and the reply was, "The President of the United States." Later, when he told his wife about the dream, she remarked that he would die in office.

Perhaps Lincoln would have survived if he had given his dream more credence and changed his plans. Perhaps he would not have visited Ford's Theatre and not been shot by John Wilkes Booth, changing the course of history. Most psychic people believe that the future is not set and that you can change it by your actions. Precognition is a mechanism by which you gain insight into the changes you need to make.

See also: **Extra Sensory Perception (ESP)**

PREDICTION

Gnothi se auton ("Know thyself.")

INSCRIPTION, ORACLE OF DELPHI, AT THE TEMPLE OF APOLLO

It is true that dreams sometimes tell the future, but please think twice before passing on a dream prophecy to another person. Remember that sometimes your own hopes and fears about the future also play a role in dreams. You may want the future to turn out a certain way, or you may fear that it will. These hopes and anxieties can be reflected in the dream content. Dreams about your own or another's personal future may be influenced by your hopes and fears.

When people come to see me for a psychic consultation, I remind myself that sitters do not wish to know their future or have it predicted. Their future could be a very sad future, and nobody wants to hear that. The truth is that they want to be told that everything is going to work out the way they wish.

Good psychic practice is not to predict but, instead, to advise people about the best course to take in order to come to the most satisfactory conclusion. When you make a prediction to someone, you wield tremendous power. The same is true when someone makes a prediction about your life. Even if you know that the person making the prediction is a charlatan, the prediction may still worry you. Predictions have a power that is similar to superstition: we don't believe them, but in the back of our mind something says "... but what if it is true?" In this way, we are disempowered by our worries. This may even cause bad things to happen to us out of sheer fright.

I have seen many people badly misguided by frightening predictions even though the "psychic" meant well. Predictions about money, health, and relationships may lead to feelings of fear of what will happen and disappointment when things do not work out as forecast.

So what should psychics do when a person comes to them for advice? Our role has to be to guide people and to help them make the best decisions to bring good fortune into their lives. We are like map readers. We see the lay of the land and, based on this, we give advice about the best thing to do. We do not say what will happen but what the person can do to make the best choices. I advise you to apply these same criteria when sharing a psychic dream with your friends and family.

In ancient Greece, the Temple of Apollo housed the famous Oracle of Delphi. Located in a dramatic setting on the south slope of Mount Parnassos, Delphi was regarded in antiquity as the center of the world. Within its walls sat the Pythia, an elderly priestess of Apollo. She made strange prophecies while in a sleepy euphoria induced by the intoxicants that emanated from water bubbling out of a rock fissure beneath the temple. (Some theorize that these gases included methane and ethane, which can be intoxicating, as well as ethylene, widely used as an anesthetic in the first half of the Twentieth century.)

The unintelligible uttering of the Pythia were interpreted by the temple priests and then composed into verses. The oracle's chief shortcoming was the ambiguity of her advice. Croesus, king of Lydia, went to war against Cyrus of Persia after the oracle told him that "a great nation would fall" if he crossed the Halys River. Unfortunately, the great nation turned out to be his own.

See also: **Future, Precognition**

PROPHECY

For God speaketh once, yea twice, yet man perceiveth it not. In a dream, a vision of the night, when deep sleep falleth upon men slumbering upon their bed, then He openeth their ears and sealeth in their instructions.

JOB 33:14-16

Dreams speak to us in the language of symbolism. They use metaphor and allegory to express our inner condition. Although nobody knows for certain why we dream, it is generally accepted that dreams stop the emotions from overheating, respond to our bodily and psychological needs, and offer solutions to our problems. And very occasionally, dreams fulfill their objectives using clairvoyant insight.

Do not jump to frightening conclusions when interpreting the meaning of a dream. Not everything in a dream is a prophecy. It is more likely that the dream is speaking about your emotions and fears than predicting events that will come to pass.

SIGNS, STORIES, EXPERIMENTS, AND SYMBOLS

Dreams have been interpreted as prophecies of the future throughout time by all civilizations. Here are a few of the main Western beliefs:

The Babylonians: For the peoples of Mesopotamia, dreams came from either the gods or demons. If a demon brought a bad dream prophecy, the Babylonian priests would pray to Mamu, the god of dreams, and ask that the bad dream never come true. Mamu was pictured as male or female, but was usually pictured as the daughter of the Sumerian sun god Utu.

The Assyrians: The Assyrians believed dreams were mostly omens of good or ill luck. Bad dreams demanded action, such as an exorcism. Other dreams were seen as advice. In fact, this sense of a misfortune being predicted by bad dreams was common to most ancient cultures.

The Egyptians: The Egyptians believed that the gods showed themselves in dreams, demanding pious acts or warning of impending doom. A dream could serve as an oracle and bring messages from the gods. The best way to get an answer to a question, including ones about health, was to incubate a dream (see **Incubation** section).

The Greeks: The Greeks also believed that the gods brought dreams and prophecies. Hypnos governed sleep. This god of sleep was the brother of Thanatos, the god of death and the father of Morpheus, the god of dreams. The early Greeks thought that the people who inhabited their dreams lived near the Underworld. Homer reports on Agamemnon's dream from Zeus carried by Hermes. It was the battle plan that came from the Demios Oneiron, the village of dreams on the way to Hades.

The Hebrews: Because their religion was monotheistic, the ancient Hebrews believed that prophetic dreams came only from the one God.

Muslims: Dreams and astrology are closely related in Muslim culture. True dreams come from Allah; false ones come from the devil, Iblis.

The Romans: The prophetic value of dreams was so important to the Romans that the Emperor Augustus decreed that anyone who had a dream about the state must proclaim it in the marketplace. Homer and Herodotus thought it natural that the gods should send dreams to men, even to deceive them, if need be, for the accomplishment of their higher ends. Julius Caesar's decision to cross the Rubicon is attributed to a dream in which he saw himself in bed with his mother (Mother Rome, the seers told him). His assassination was foretold in his wife's dream: "She held him in her arms, bleeding, and stabbed." Another Caesar, Caesar Augustus, is said to have walked the streets as a beggar because of instructions he received in a dream.

See also: **Future, Precognition, Prediction, Time**

PROTECTION

A ruffled mind makes a restless pillow.

CHARLOTTE BRONTË, BRITISH AUTHOR

Practitioners of psychic and magical dreams believe that you should protect yourself from negative influences while sleeping. These influences may be malevolent spirits or the negative thoughts and energies that may be projected toward you by other people. They claim that when people are in the highly sensitive state of psychic dreaming, they experience an increased vulnerability to negative influences, so some form of psychic self-defense is necessary.

Herbal teas are believed to protect you during sleep and also to induce psychic dreams. Herbal teas help you relax and enter the dream state, especially when they are prepared with the intention of triggering psychic dreams. Chamomile is a good tea to help you relax, and valerian brings deep sleep, acting as a sedative. Lavender or myrrh oil applied to the temples before you retire is soothing, can aid restful sleep, and is believed to protect against nightmares or negative influences.

Skullcap herbal tea is said to stimulate dream states and memory. Mugwort oil applied a few hours before sleep can be used in combination with this remedy to increase vivid and lucid dreams. A suitable fragrance for this sort of work is sandalwood, which is said to safeguard you if you are working with clairvoyance. Some people may benefit from protective symbols kept close to the bed. Crosses, pentagrams, stars of David, and runes placed near the bed or beneath the pillow lend their protective properties to you while you are in the dream state.

Native American dreamcatchers are a popular way to prevent nightmares. These weblike nets are hung above the bed to catch bad dreams, granting you only pleasant dreams. It is generally accepted that dreamcatchers were first used by the Ojibwa tribe and then spread out among other Algonquin tribes. They were originally used to protect children from nightmares. Good dreams pass through the web, but bad dreams get caught in them. Similarly, in the voodoo tradition, dream bowls are kept under the bed to stop bad dreams. The protective power of a bowl is increased if you fill it with a few drops of brandy or anisette. If you have trouble sleeping or have persistent nightmares, add valerian root directly to the spirit bowl. When you pour out the solution in the morning, the bad dreams go down the drain with it.

SIGNS, STORIES, EXPERIMENTS, AND SYMBOLS

To keep away nightmares and encourage prophetic dreams, some people like to use herbal pillows. Depending upon which herbs you include, you can use an herbal pillow for protection or to trigger a psychic dream. Place the pillow beneath your normal pillow.

Psychic Dream Pillow

4 oz. dried lavender flowers
4 oz. dried sage
4 oz. deer's tongue herb
2 oz. hops
4 oz. coltsfoot herb
4 oz. sweet fern
2 oz. wood violet

As a psychic dreamer, you may also be interested in the Sky Walking Dream Pillow, which is said to induce astral travel.

Sky Walking Dream Pillow

1 part jasmine

$\frac{1}{8}$ part cloves and cinnamon

2 parts mugwort

2 parts sweet woodruff

1 part willow (dried leaves from tree)

5 drops Frankincense essential oil

5 drops myrrh essential oil

2 drops chamomile

5 drops nutmeg

PSYCHIC ATTACKS

Certain rash people have asserted that, just as there are no mice where there are no cats, so no one is possessed where there are no exorcists.

GEORG CHRISTOPH LICHTENBERG,
GERMAN PHILOSOPHER

Throughout history, people have reported being attacked by evil spirits in their sleep. In particular, Christianity has traditionally taught that **Satan** and his hordes of **demons** roam about the world attempting to harm people. Many theologians believe that these ideas, which took hold in the first century, predate Christianity by many centuries. They may have originated in the Zoroastrian faith of Persia during the period of Babylonian captivity. Fortunately, liberal Christians have long abandoned belief in demons.

Nonetheless, the theme of demonic psychic attack makes excellent movies and probably is at the heart of people's worries about this issue. The vast majority of the cases I have investigated have psychological causes and have more to do with obsession than possession. In most instances, the "attack" is the result of an overactive imagination. The mind is a powerful tool, and the unconscious can play tricks. In other words, there is no external entity involved. If a psychic tells a person that he is possessed, the unconscious mind will oblige. In more serious cases of mental imbalance, the cause may be an early symptom of schizophrenia, and it is advisable to seek professional help.

Most mediums believe that **mischievous spirits** can occasionally take advantage of the mentally disturbed but cannot physically possess a person. There is only room for one spirit in the physical body.

In addition to being attacked by spirits, people may also believe themselves to be attacked by negative energies, such as those that arise because of a curse or from witchcraft. The best way to protect yourself from all forms of psychic attack is simply to have no fear. People who have faith in themselves and their personal power cannot be harmed by any external influence. Some people find chants, magical amulets, and prayer to be helpful, but the function of all these things is to dispel fear and restore your spiritual stability. They are only props. Also, remember that whatever your religion, the power of God is omnipresent. All you need to do is open yourself to this great power of compassion, and you will have invincible psychic protection.

A real or imagined magical amulet may give psychic protection during sleep.

In earlier times, people believed that fallen angels known as **Incubus** and **Succubus** could sexually assault a sleeping person. An Incubus is a male demon who comes to sleeping women and attempts to rape them. The female equivalent is the Succubus. The man who succumbs to a Succubus will not awaken from sleep. Intercourse with these spirits was thought to be the cause for the birth of demons, witches, and deformed children. Mothers of deformed children were often put to death. Sometimes, the children fathered by these demons were believed to have magical powers. For example, in the Arthurian legend, the magician Merlin was the result of an Incubus copulating with his mother.

In less permissive times than ours, the Incubus and Succubus were used to account for the fact that people had "improper" dreams of which they might feel ashamed.

See also: **Paralysis**

PSYCHOKINESIS

Mind over batter.

VIVIAN STANSHALL, BRITISH ARTIST AND PERFORMER

Psychokinesis is the word used by parapsychologists for the paranormal influence of the mind on physical events and processes. It is the power of the mind to influence matter—to move objects by thought, for example. Uri Geller claims he can bend spoons, stop watches, and use his mind to make pencils roll across a table by an act of will.

Although dreams may not bend spoons, perhaps they can generate an energy that influences the world around us. It is my belief that the nature of our thoughts can change the world around us. Negative thoughts attract bad things, whereas optimistic and cheerful thoughts promote good fortune and healing. During dreams, you are working on another level of reality. It may be that dreams influence upcoming situations and attract so-called good or bad luck. If this is true, then our dreams are influencing events, which would be an example of mind over matter or, more correctly, psychokinesis.

I have been sent one or two cases in which people have dreamed of doing something and discovered the next day that what they dreamed happened in reality. One woman wrote to me to say that she dreamed of tying a purple ribbon around a tree. In the morning, she went downstairs to find a purple ribbon tied to her banister. Nobody could explain how it got there. My thought is that maybe the woman sleepwalks—she claims that this is not the case—or perhaps the ribbon was there before and had been spotted by her subconscious. Maybe someone tied the ribbon in place, and she "saw" it in her dream. Nonetheless, she claims that this is not the case and insists that the dream appears to have materialized a ribbon.

See also: **Clairvoyance, Extra Sensory Perception (ESP), Parapsychology, Precognition, Telepathy**

REMOTE VIEWING (RV)

The Truth Is Out There.

THE X FILES, TELEVISION SHOW

Remote viewing occurs when a person "sees" a distant location, object, or event using extra sensory perception. It works whether the target is in the next room or on the other side of the world. Remote viewing can sometimes occur during deep meditation, trance, or sleep.

Remote viewing in dreams may occur during lucid dreaming. Some psychics believe that the dream body separates from the physical body and travels in the body of light to the actual location. Others say that it is only the consciousness that is projected. Whatever the truth, somehow we can view other places and at times bring back verifiable information to prove that our experience is true.

New York artist and psychic Ingo Swann performed the first pioneering experiments under the auspices of the American Society for Psychical Research. Eventually, Swann teamed up with Dr. Hal Puthoff at SRI-International's Radio Physics Laboratory in Menlo Park, California. They coined the term "remote viewing."

During the Cold War, the CIA used Ingo Swann and other clairvoyants to act as psychic spies. Experiments to use remote viewing to observe Soviet military installations began at the Stanford Research Institute in 1972. Of course, the government was very interested in the experiments because no type of shielding can prevent a properly trained remote viewer from gaining access to the desired target. If this were proven to be true, it would be the perfect form of spying.

However, they had to act quickly because they knew that the Russians were undertaking similar research.

When the CIA lost interest, General Edmund R. Thompson and General Albert N. Stubblebine, along with Congressmen Claiborne Pell, and Charlie Rose, and an influential Senate staffer named Richard D'Amato continued the research under the Pentagon's budget.

But as the Cold War melted in 1994, the government found it difficult to justify the spending. In addition, some of the experiments being undertaken, such as searching for the Ark of the Covenant using RV, were a little too esoteric for some congressmen. The project was eventually canceled in 1995; in its final incarnation, it was called "Star Gate."

SIGNS, STORIES, EXPERIMENTS, AND SYMBOLS

Some tips to develop your remote viewing skills during sleep:

Choosing Targets: Serious researchers choose targets that include geographic locations, hidden objects, archaeological sites, and space objects. If you set up a dream experiment with others, you will need to be able to verify your accuracy by selecting targets that can be checked. (See the "remote viewing exercise" in **Clairvoyance.**)

Senses: Research has found that remote viewing also involves mental impressions pertaining to the other senses, such as sounds, tastes, smells, and textures. Make a note of all these things when you wake up. In some cases, your impressions may simply be an intuitive "knowing."

Recording: In the lab, the remote viewer verbalizes what he or she is perceives. In addition, the viewer may write notes, draw sketches, and even produce three-dimensional models to express the results of the remote viewing episode, or "session." You may wish to learn from the research and use a cassette recorder, a sketchbook, and a dream diary to record your remote-viewing dreams.

Safeguards: If you would like to set up serious sessions with your friends, you will need to include a number of safeguards. Sessions in the lab should be conducted in a setting that prevents knowledge of the target from "leaking" to the viewer. These safeguards are important to ensure that the viewer does not receive hints or clues about the target in any way other than through ESP.

Common Sense: Remote viewing is a serious scientific discipline. It is not to be used for giving "psychic readings."

See also: **Clairvoyance, Journeys, Lucid Dreams, Out-of-Body Experiences (OBEs)**

SERIALISM

As I become activated enough to lose my sense of ego-identity, then conventional time loses its meaning, and I get caught up with extra-dimensional adventures in the future.

ALAN VAUGHAN, CLAIRVOYANT

Psychic dreaming was first popularized through the writings of J.W. Dunne, author of *An Experiment with Time* as well as other books. Dunne proposed that our minds roam through time during sleep, and he cited many examples of his own psychic dreams.

Dunne kept detailed records of his dreams. He would regularly look back over his notes to see if any dreams reflected incidents in his own life or events that had not yet happened at the time of the dream but occurred later on. He discovered that many of his dreams predicted the future, and from these examples he developed a theory of time which he called serialism.

Dunne believed that his theory of serialism explained psychic and precognitive dreams. We all assume that time travels in a straight line, but according to Dunne, it is like a stretched cord or a tangled skein of wool. He also proposed that your ordinary self, which he called Observer 1, is confined to the present "now," which lives in a time frame from birth to death, like a long length of wool. In sleep, another aspect of yourself, Observer 2, is active and roams at will through the skein of time. Hence, dreams about the future are not precognitive to Observer 2 because in this state everything has already taken place.

Dunne's interesting ideas from the early 1900s correspond with many of the latest theories of time and space being proposed by physicists today.

SIGNS, STORIES, EXPERIMENTS, AND SYMBOLS

Between 1900 and 1902, Dunne had a series of dreams that appeared to predict world events. Most of these were about disasters. Perhaps the most striking of these dreams was the one he had well in advance of the volcanic eruption of May 8, 1902. This eruption destroyed St. Pierre, the main trading center of the island of Martinique and killed 40,000 people.

See also: **Time**

SKEPTICISM

X rays are a hoax.

LORD KELVIN, BRITISH ENGINEER
AND PHYSICIST

Skeptics believe that psychic dreams are mainly anecdotal and rely on the word of the person who claims to have had the dream. They argue that only occasionally has a dream been told to someone else before the events take place. It is rare to find a record of a psychic dream of the future that was described to independent witnesses before rather than after the event occurred. Of course, the dream may just be a coincidence, because the unconscious holds a great deal more knowledge about our surroundings and possible events than we suppose. Your unconscious may pick up clues about a possible danger during the day, and this information may be woven into the fabric of your dreams. For example, your unconscious may spot a dangerous stairway even though you do not consciously notice it. You dream of falling down the stairs, and it actually happens in real life. You may naturally assume the dream was a prophecy of the future, and yet the mind contained this information all along.

Although skeptics may scoff at the predictions of the future, many predictions have been well documented and do appear to anticipate upcoming events. The literature of parapsychology is huge, and there are a great many parapsychology journals and thousands of books in the Library of Congress. However, we almost never see any mention of all these immense labors in serious science magazines or journals. Most mainstream scientists refuse to examine the evidence for psychic dreams based on logical positivism.

This concept states that the only acceptable observations are those that can be experienced by all persons, and we don't all claim to have precognitive dreams. The rules of science would have to be changed if psychic dreaming were to be accepted by traditional science. Indeed, if paranormal phenomena were proved to be true, the fundamental materialist assumptions of science would be turned on their heads.

Skeptics fear that proof of the existence of any psi phenomena leads to a medieval superstitious mentality, which will in turn support a rising tide of dangerous, primitive thinking. My guess is that what really frightens these scientists is the daunting prospect of giving up their cherished beliefs.

SIGNS, STORIES, EXPERIMENTS, AND SYMBOLS

How would the skeptics explain away how murderer William Corder came to his undoing by way of a dream?

In 1827, Maria Marten of England eloped with Corder, a local farmer, but something was not quite right. After several months, the girl's parents began to wonder why they had not heard from their daughter. Corder reassured his in-laws that Maria was quite safe and well and that he had "placed her at some distance lest his friends might discover the fact of his marriage and exhibit displeasure at the circumstance." He claimed that she was living on the Isle of Wight, but letters they supposedly received from her always bore a London postmark.

On three successive nights in March of 1828, Maria's mother dreamed that her daughter had been murdered and buried in a part of Corder's premises called the Red Barn.

She was so convinced that her dream was true that on Saturday, April 19, 1828, she persuaded her husband to apply for legal permission to examine the Red Barn in order to look for their daughter's clothes. He dug at the exact spot that had been shown to his wife in her dream and soon uncovered a blood-stained shawl. With his heart beating with fright, he dug deeper, and to his horror he raked out part of a human body. He had found his daughter's corpse in an advanced state of decomposition.

William Corder denied the crime, but he was found guilty of murder by the jury. On his return to the jail, Corder confessed to the warden that he was guilty. "I am a guilty man," he exclaimed and immediately after-wards made a full confession. Just before he was hanged, he said in a feeble tone, "I am justly sentenced, and may God forgive me!"

See also: **Symbolism**

SOULMATES

You have been mine before,—
How long ago I may not know:
But just when at that swallow's soar
Your neck turned so, Some veil did fall,—
I knew it all of yore.

DANTE GABRIEL ROSSETTI, BRITISH POET

Could it be that in dreams we may discover soulmate connections between ourselves and our partners? These dreams may reveal past lives that we have shared together and our future destiny together. Some dreams show our connection symbolically. For example, I often dream of living in Tibet as a yogi. In one particular dream, a book falls from the sky and lands on my crossed legs. The monks around me get very excited and say this is an auspicious sign. They tell me that I must prepare for a new life, and they begin to chant an uplifting mantra. Next, I am with my wife, Jane, and we are looking forward to what may lie ahead. A guru figure explains that we are at the source of the Ganges and must now swim the river, but warns that it will be very cold.

The Ganges is the holy Indian **river** in which the ashes of the dead are scattered in the hope of being taken to a fortunate future life. The icy waters shown in my dream may symbolize the coldness of the corpse and death itself. Crossing a river is a common symbol for the transition to the next life and is found in Western symbolism in figures such as the Greek **boatman**, Charon, who ferries the dead across the river Styx to Hades. In this dream, the source of the river is shown. In a psychic dream, a **spring**, a **fountain**, or the source of a river may show the source of life itself from which awareness springs. These symbols can show the life-giving power of the unconscious and, in this case, point to some of the primary objectives of my life. In a symbolic way, the dream shows that my life and that of my wife are intertwined at a spiritual level. I believe that this dream indicates that Jane and I are soulmates and share a common destiny.

Dreams about a soulmate may include imagery similar to the above or may even include specific details that can be verified. Before I met my wife, I would dream of being with a group of people fleeing from soldiers and wild dogs. In the nightmare, we are attacked from behind, and our heads are

Can dreams reveal the identity of your soulmate?

severed. Remarkably, Jane also had had this same dream before we met. Strangest of all is the fact that Jane, my daughter Danielle, and I all have similar birthmarks on the backs of our necks—as if our bodies were still carrying the marks of something that had happened to us in a previous life.

SIGNS, STORIES, EXPERIMENTS, AND SYMBOLS

There are cases of people who believe that their future partner has been revealed in a psychic dream. For example, during a consultation with a medium called Wendy (a pseudonym), I asked why I kept seeing a wounded soldier and a nurse from World War I. For some reason, I knew this would soon be important.

Wendy explained how she had a recurring dream about working as a nurse in a makeshift hospital close to the Somme in 1916. In the dream, she had fallen in love with one of the terminally wounded soldiers. As he died, she handed the man a red rose and promised that she would be with him when her time came to die.

Sometime after the consultation, Wendy telephoned me to explain that she had fallen in love and was planning to marry. After her fiancée had proposed, he confessed that she reminded him of a woman from his dreams. He explained to the astonished Wendy how he often dreamed of being in an army hospital and how a beautiful nurse handed him a red rose.

It would appear that dreams do sometimes identify your future partner. Nonetheless, you must try not to become the victim of your dream fantasies when you are establishing a relationship. Carl Jung believed that each of us is psychologically part male and part female. He called these two aspects of the self the **anima** (female) and the **animus** (male). In our dreams, the anima and animus appear as the perfect man and perfect woman.

When you fall in love, you may project this inner vision of the perfect man or woman onto your partner. Unfortunately, these fantasies are usually unrealistic. Newlyweds often face a crisis when they begin to distinguish between the person they thought they married and their spouse.

SPELLS

Magic has a universal appeal. I don't believe it in the way that I describe it in my books, but I'd love it to be real.

J.K. ROWLING, BRITISH AUTHOR

Today, there is a resurgence of interest in Wicca and in the art of casting spells. Modern Wicca is not like the witchcraft we see in the movies. It is a "New Age" interest and usually refers to anything created by Alexandrian or Gardnerian studies. Wicca is based on traditional witchcraft, but it is less secretive. It encourages anyone with an interest to use the ancient arts to benefit their life and influence their fortunes.

Some of the most enduring traditions focus around love and spells to entrap someone you desire or to reveal your soulmate. Dreams play an important part in this process and are used by practitioners of Wicca to gain insight into their romantic fortunes.

In many ways, spells are very similar to prayers. They are catalysts that use psychic energy to influence events by petitioning a deity. The divine part of a person's nature is activated, and this may affect the influences surrounding their lives and direction. Wiccans consider spells that use love magic or curses to harm someone to be manipulative because they infringe on the free will of another person. Spells that produce insight into events are benign and may help a person quickly find the best path.

SIGNS, STORIES, EXPERIMENTS, AND SYMBOLS

Ash Tree Love Spell

First you must pluck a sprig from an ash tree and recite the following traditional rhyme:

> *Even-ash, even-ash, I pluck thee,*
> *This night my own true love to see,*
> *Neither in his bed nor in the bare,*
> *But in the clothes he does every day wear.*

For centuries, the ash tree has been associated with fertility; therefore, it is closely associated with love and romance. Pagan societies believed that the first man was created from the branches and flesh of the ash tree. In particular, the seeds of the ash have long been used in love magic and as a means of divination. If you place your sprig beneath your pillow when the moon is full, your dreams will reveal your future lover or spouse.

Ash trees have also been associated with rebirth and eternal love. A Norwegian legend tells of Axel Thordsen and Fair Valdborg, two lovers who were unable to come together in life, but who were buried next to each other. An ash tree was planted on each grave, and as the trees grew to the same height, the branches inclined and became entwined. They became a symbol for eternal love.

Saint Agnes Love Spell

The traditional Saint Agnes love spell is similar to the ash tree love spell. Saint Agnes is one of the best known and honored of the Roman martyrs. She is a symbol of purity. Because she refused to offer incense to the goddess Minerva, a Roman judge sent her to a house of prostitution. However, when one youth attempted to molest her, he was "struck down, as if by lightning." He fell to the ground, blind.

The Saint Agnes love spell is traditionally cast on her feast day of January 21st and is supposed to show you your true love. To cast the spell, you light a pink candle before retiring to bed. Hold a mirror to your face and say:

"Dear Saint Agnes, sweet and fair, I call upon thee with humble prayer. With clarity I pray to see the face of my true love to be. Tonight let him be dream revealed, with a kiss this rhyme be sealed."

Thanking Saint Agnes, you then kiss the mirror and place it under your pillow, glass side up. Your dreams will show you the face of your soulmate.

See also: **Wicca and Witchcraft**

SUCCESS

Success comes to those that dare to dream dreams and are foolish enough to try and make them come true.

SABEER BHATIA, FOUNDER OF HOTMAIL

Some people may consider dreams—and particularly supposedly psychic dreams—to be a load of rubbish. Yet, many of the most creative and powerful people in history owe their success to inspiration they received in dreams. Dreams have foretold the future, inspired great works of art, and changed the course of history.

SIGNS, STORIES, EXPERIMENTS, AND SYMBOLS

There are many examples of famous psychic dreams in this book. Here are a few that may have changed the course of history:

Many people who achieve greatness owe part of their success to the inventive, intuitive, and predictive power of dreams. It was in a dream that a goat herder named Temujin was shown that he would rise in stature to become Genghis Khan, one of the greatest leaders of all time, with an empire stretching from China to Russia. Throughout his life Genghis Khan would call upon his dreams and from them would receive his battle plans. Similarly, Alexander the Great dreamed that he saw a satyr, a woodland god. He chased and caught the satyr. His advisor Aristander told him it was a good omen, because the Greek word for satyr ($\Sigma\alpha\tau\theta\rho o\Omega$) was an anagram (considered auspicious by the Greeks) for "Tyre is yours" ($\Sigma\alpha$ T$\theta\rho o\Omega$). The dream inspired him to escalate the war, which he won.

General George McClelland, during the American Civil War, had a dream about the ghost of George Washington rolling out a map of the troop positions of the Confederates preparing for a march on Washington. General McClelland is reported to have taken notes on the presentation and won the battle. Many other great leaders listened to their dreams in this way. The angels St. Catherine, St. Margaret, and St. Michael populated the dreams of Joan of Arc and revealed to her the way to wage successful military campaigns. In a waking vision she correctly foresaw that an arrow in the impending battle for Orleans would wound her.

Success in the arts has also been attributed to dreams. The dreams of many great artists have been touched by the Muse. Some artists have the talent of bringing the power of dreaming into the waking state and claim to fall into a kind of somnambulism when they work. When this happens the artist becomes merely the instrument of the unconscious powers that express themselves through him or her. Picasso claimed that "Painting is stronger than I am; it makes me do what it wants."

Many writers believe that their literary successes have been aided by vivid dreams. William Wordsworth's greatest poems, he said were inspired by dreams, as was "Kubla Khan," by Samuel Taylor Coleridge. Jules Verne's visions of the future were inspired by dreams, as were the characters in many of the stories by Charles Dickens. Robert Louis Stevenson claimed that his best stories came directly from his dreams, including the theme for *Dr. Jekyll and Mr. Hyde*. As a child, Stevenson suffered from nightmares and learned to control his dreams to change the nightmares. Many of his descriptions suggest that Stevenson was a lucid dreamer who used dreams to revise his plays and stories while asleep.

Throughout history, dreams have been the initiator of many great discoveries and have opened the doors to success for creative men and women. Elias Howe invented the lock-stitch sewing machine based on a dream of savages holding spears with holes in the blades, which showed him where to place the eye of the needle. D. B. Parkinson's dream about war lead to the invention of the Bell Lab's M9 gun director, which brought down the V-1 buzz bombs launched toward England in World War II. Neils Bohr identified the physical structure of atom as a result of a dream about the planets circling the sun, and the 1936 Nobel Prize in physiology was awarded to Otto Leowi for an experiment that he first saw in a dream.

But perhaps the greatest discovery for many reading this book was what happened to Christopher Columbus. He dreamed he heard someone speak to him with the message, "God will give thee the keys of the ocean." The dream inspired him to pursue his scheme for a voyage westward and to the eventual discovery of the New World.

SUPERSTITION

We are such stuff as dreams are made on; and our little life is rounded with a sleep.

WILLIAM SHAKESPEARE, PLAYWRIGHT

Since the earliest times, people have believed that dreams hold special messages. People believed that dreams contained prophecies that augured good or bad fortune. Many of the meanings given to dreams were taken from the existing omens associated with nature, such as the hooting of **owls** or the howling of **dogs**, which were considered to predict forth-coming events. For example, to dream of a barking dog indicated that there would be quarrels; if it bites you, someone will betray you. The Chinese say that dreaming of dogs foretells fights and disruption, and if a dog enters the house, a field worker will die. Similarly, Native Americans believe that screeching **owls** predict death. The same superstition can be found in European cultures where hooting owls, or any noisy night birds, are generally considered to be bad omens, unless the person is single, in which case, he or she will marry an intelligent person.

Unusual events, such as **eclipses**, **comets**, or the flights of sacred **birds**, were believed to be messages from the gods. These folklore themes became part of the predictive dream traditions. To dream of an eclipse is a bad omen because it indicates that you may lose a female friend. (The moon is a traditional female symbol.) Comets were a worrying deviation from the order of nature and were considered to be portents of evil. They were thought to be a symbol of war or of shattered dreams when seen in dreams. A dream of flights of birds signifies lawsuits and enemies.

Superstition is any belief that has no basis in fact. The belief usually pertains to a cause-and-effect relationship, such as the belief that spilling **salt** will cause bad luck. The life of a superstitious person is a path fraught with danger. If you think that all you have to worry about are magpies and spilled salt, think again; everyday life and dreams, too, are beset with thousands of potential terrors.

(Knock on wood; you will not let super-stition get in the way of your enjoyment of your psychic dreams.)

SIGNS, STORIES, EXPERIMENTS, AND SYMBOLS

According to superstition, it is unlucky to go against the advice of a dream. This may well be true for many of your dreams, for they often have a superior insight into who you are and what motivates you. Also they may see into the future. This is the reason the famous psychic Edgar Cayce said that you should always act on your dreams, even if you don't understand a dream's meaning.

But dream superstition has also been used to wield political influence by playing on a person's superstition that they must obey dreams. In medieval times, dreams were sometimes used as a sanction for those wishing to put forward controversial political policies. One of the most notable cases concerned the knight who informed King Henry II that the voices of St. Peter and the Archangel Gabriel had told him to present a number of demands foreshadowing the Magna Carta. Similarly, how far would Joan of Arc have advanced if her French followers had not trusted her dreams and visions?

Throughout the ages, dreams have spoken with the authority to make political decisions or even to identify criminals.

See also: **Omens, Oneiromancy**

SYMBOLISM

A little learning is a dangerous thing; drink deep or taste not of the Pierian Spring.

ALEXANDER POPE, BRITISH POET

If you dream of a terrible event, do you jump to conclusions and assume it is a prophecy of doom? My mailbag is full of letters from worried readers who believe that their dreams predict terrible events for them and the world at large. Judging by the number of people who write to me, if these dreams were all to come true, no one would be left on the planet.

Clearly, not every dream about the future is a prediction. A skeptic will point out that since we all dream between three and four times a night and since everyone dreams, it is likely someone somewhere was dreaming about a news event before it happened. For example, it is likely that someone somewhere was dreaming an airplane crashed into a high-rise building just before the 9/11 disaster took place.

Skeptics also argue that precognitive dreams only come true because you selectively remember your dreams that come true but don't remember those that don't. Thus, you attribute your dreams to psychic precognition. Of course, many people assume that dreams are just random thoughts and images. They reject all the convincing evidence for psychic phenomena, such as the extensive research into telepathy using the Ganzfeld experiments, the remote viewing and precognition data from the Stanford Research Institute and other research labs, and the rock-solid evidence for ESP and psychokinesis in the research from Princeton University.

Nonetheless, it is best not to assume that all dreams are psychic dreams. Nobody knows what purpose dreams serve, but most psychologists agree that dreams are a link between your conscious mind and your unconscious. They believe that dreams use symbolism to express thoughts, feelings, and emotions. In this way, your dreams are an emotional safety valve. Without them, your frustrations and anxieties would overwhelm you. Your dreams about disasters, for example, may have less to do with the world at large and more to do with the emotional disasters and disappointments that have been happening in your own life. They speak of the hurt and shock you feel when things go wrong now. Your dreams may also recall the emotional pain you have known in the past.

In addition, dreams may also have something to do with your ability to learn. They help you assimilate what happens to you. They organize the events of the day and reassess them. Dreams show you solutions to your problems and prepare you for the future. In doing this, they expose your deepest fears and indicate ways to inner peace. Dreams may speak literally and give you a direct glimpse into the future, but in most instances they are a representation of your thoughts, ideas, worries, hopes, and fears shown in symbols, metaphors, and images. Use discernment when you interpret a dream as a portent of the future. Of course, some are portents, but you should consider whether your dream has a symbolic meaning before assuming it is paranormal.

Prior to modern psychology, people used to believe that the images from a dream were portents. Today, many dream books still draw on these superstitions. I have included some of these old prophetic meanings in this book and have explained their origins in more detail in the **Oneiromancy** section. Needless to say, these old superstitions need to be taken with a very large grain of salt. Also, many ancient dream interpretations may be lost on modern man. For example, some ancient dream interpretations were based on punning, or verbal connections between similar words. In ancient Egyptian, the words for "donkey" and "great" were homonyms; therefore, a dream about eating donkey meat meant good luck. Some of these old ideas—many of which date back to

the library of the Egyptian scribe Kenhirkhopeshef—have been passed down through the generations and continue to appear in modern dream books.

Many people still believe that the ancient dream books were right and that all dream images have specific messages about the future. It is my belief that most of these are nonsense, but I have included many examples because many people believe them. Readers who don't, will find them an amusing diversion.

SIGNS, STORIES, EXPERIMENTS, AND SYMBOLS

Although every dream is unique, people have many dreams in common. These dreams usually highlight things people worry about. Below are listed the ten most common dreams, their symbolic meanings, and what they may be saying about your future.

Dreams of Being Chased

This very common dream usually occurs when there is an issue that you don't want to face. You are literally running away from a problem. This dream may be a metaphor for insecurities about circumstances closing in on you, or you may be at the mercy of feelings that get out of control.

Psychic dream meaning: This dream is most likely dealing with issues that are already a problem for you. It may relate to worries from past hurts or to traumas from childhood. To be successful in the future, you will first need to deal with the issues that you refuse to address today.

Dreams of Falling

As a symbol, falling highlights a loss of emotional equilibrium or self-control. You may fear "letting go" in real life. This dream may represent your insecurity, a fear of failure, or an inability to cope with a situation. In relation to your career, this dream may show that your anxiety is preventing you from progressing. Sometimes, this dream can be triggered by a drop in blood pressure as you fall asleep.

Psychic dream meaning: You may have anxieties about your ability to cope with future situations. This dream may also be the onset of an out-of-body experience. Most people describe a sensation of rising above the body when this happens. However, I have spoken to people who say that an OBE begins with a feeling of falling through the bed.

Dreams of Going to Work Only Partially Dressed or Naked

This dream shows your anxieties about feeling vulnerable. You may be feeling emotionally sensitive. The dream can show that you have a big secret or something to hide. The dream may show the "naked truth" about you. You may have feelings of being exposed or ridiculed. In relation to work, this dream may show that you feel that you are not up to the job.

Psychic dream meaning: This is probably a symbolic dream, so don't expect to find yourself nude in public. If you are training to become more psychic, you may find that as your sensitivity increases you feel vulnerable to negative vibrations and may be easily drained by the people around you. Eventually, this feeling will disappear as you gain control over the gift and understand how to shield yourself from unwanted vibrational influences.

Dream of Having to Address a Large Audience

Often you will dream of suddenly discovering that you must give a speech, as in the film *The Third Man*. This is another anxiety dream. It shows that you feel you are unprepared, and its theme is similar to the exposed feeling in the naked dream above. You may be unprepared emotionally for what is happening in your life, or a work issue may be worrying you. These issues are in the spotlight.

Psychic dream meaning: If you learn the right strategic and tactical techniques, you may be able to address your worries about being the center of attention, particularly if this relates to a work issue. The dream may be triggered by planned events that you are not ready for. Look at the rest of the content in the dream to see if you can find hints for the solutions to the problem. Your dream may include people and scenarios that give a clairvoyant hint about whom to ask and what to do.

Dreams of Problems with Computers, Cars, and Other Equipment

These dreams are more common nowadays. They are a symbol that your life may be going wrong. Perhaps you have had an emotional upset, or the dream may be literal. Your subconscious may be struggling to solve a software problem that you could not fix while at work.

Psychic dream meaning: I have had these dreams and then found that the car will not start or there's a software crash. So, they are not always symbolic. In one instance, a dream about a computer crash also gave me the way to fix the problem. Dreams are an incredible tool for working out problems, and sometimes they draw on information that can only be accessed using clairvoyance.

Dreams About Taking Exams

This dream says you feel the same anxiety you did when you were at school taking exams. This may be a dream that expresses a fear of failure that may have originated in childhood stemming from fear of punishment or withdrawal of love. Other related themes may include dreams about missing trains or being late for work.

Psychic dream meaning: The psychic Edgar Cayce advised that a person should act on a dream even if it was symbolic. So, brush up on your skills and set the alarm a little earlier if you have an important date scheduled.

Teeth Falling Out

This dream is a symbol for insecurity that often comes at a time of transition in your life. It expresses feelings that are similar to the insecurity children feel when their milk teeth fall out, and they approach maturity. It may show your anxiety about a new job or relationship. You may be preventing yourself from becoming happy and successful.

Psychic dream meaning: This dream means that you are going to wake up one morning with a set of gums instead of teeth, and flippers where your feet were. Sorry, just joking. This is a symbolic dream. Chinese superstition says that a dream about teeth falling out is an augury that money is coming to you. To become successful, you must let go of fear and allow changes to come into your life when necessary.

Dreams of Snakes

In dreams, snakes often symbolize fear and are associated with the Christian symbol for evil. They are also a phallic symbol and may represent a fear of sexuality. Yet the snake may also represent spiritual transformation because they shed their skins. The people of some cultures believe snakes represent rebirth. Medicine's symbol, the caduceus, is two snakes entwined on a staff. It comes from the ancient Greeks' belief that snakes had healing powers.

Psychic dream meaning: You have the power to transform your life. This dream shows the need for change. Consider whether this dream may include medical prognosis. From a spiritual/psychic standpoint, this dream may show the awakening of your spiritual powers. In the East, they speak of the Kundalini energy from the base of the spine that rises through the chakras to the crown of the head. The Kundalini energy is represented by a coiled snake. When it awakens, so do spiritual powers.

Dreams of Death

Dreams of death are symbolic. They represent the ending of one phase so that a new one can begin. The person who has died in the dream may represent an aspect of yourself. For example, if someone you love has died, the dream may indicate that you have lost touch with the romantic part of your own nature. If you see yourself as the corpse, this may show that you can't cope with your problems. In relation to work, it may mean that you are "buried" under a mountain of work.

Psychic dream meaning: These dreams are usually symbolic and are not a cause for concern. The theme has been covered in detail in the **Death** entry of this book.

Dreams of Flying

These dreams are generally very pleasant. Freud saw flying dreams as a symbol of sexual release. The dream also shows release from problems and anxieties. When your dreaming spirit soars, it means that you've been liberated from an obstruction in your life. It may show that you have high hopes and are overcoming obstacles at last.

Psychic dream meaning: This shows that you are overcoming your problems and tensions. It may also show the onset of an out-of-body experience. (*See* **Out-of-Body Experiences**.)

See also: **Introduction, Oneiromancy, Skepticism**

TELEPATHY

I think we dream so we don't have to be apart so long. If we're in each other's dreams, we can be together all the time.

BILL WATTERSON, CARTOONIST

In a telepathic dream, the dreamer receives messages from someone else or from someone else's dreams. Sometimes, the dreamer seems to pick up someone else's thoughts and expresses them as a dream. Included in this category are dreams of spirits, ghosts, and those recently dead, who "speak" to you using telepathy.

Telepathy occurs in dreams when thoughts, emotions, or physical sensations are transmitted from one mind to another. They have been widely studied by scientists because, of all the forms of psychic dreaming, they are comparatively easy to verify. Inasmuch as telepathic dreams involve both a receiver and a sender, experiments can be set up to test the phenomena by noting how a receiver's dreams are influenced by thoughts intentionally sent to him while sleeping.

The Italian psychical researcher G.B.

Ermacora pioneered dream telepathy experiments in the 1880s. They were published in the proceedings of the American Society for Psychical Research in 1889. Ermacora worked with a medium named Maria Manzini as his main subject. Although they achieved some very remarkable results, the experiments did not have the controls and safeguards we would expect of a serious scientific investigation. Nonetheless, Ermacora made the first serious attempt at inducing dream telepathy. Some of these ideas were developed further in the 1940s by a young Viennese psychologist named Wilfrid Dain whose work was taken seriously by some members of the scientific community and published in Duke University's *Parapsychology Bulletin.*

The most important advances were made at the Maimonides Institute in Brooklyn, New York, by a team of parapsychologists including Montague Ullman, Stanley Krippner, Alan Vaughan, and Charles Honorton. The Maimonides team was funded for ten years to study dream telepathy. Their techniques involved monitoring sleeping subjects' brain waves and eye movements and then waking the subjects to get an immediate report about their dreams. In another room, the telepathic "senders" concentrated on target pictures designed to create a particular impression. The "receivers'" dreams often contained fragments of the imagery or emotional content similar to the picture being transmitted. Montague Ullman commented that if a subject's dream "is vivid, colored...and somewhat puzzling to the dreamer and does not 'fit' into his dream pattern or reflect recent activity, then we can be alerted to the possibility that the dream is being influenced by ESP."

The biggest telepathic transmission test

was conducted in 1971. Two thousand people who were attending a Grateful Dead rock concert were asked to focus on a color slide and attempt to send the image by telepathy to the dream laboratory 45 miles away in Brooklyn. Here, the psychic Malcolm Bessent was asleep and would attempt to reach out to the concert and receive the images in his dream over six nights. Stanley Krippner, from the Maimonides team, pointed out that many of the revelers at the concert were already in altered states of consciousness from the ingestion of psychedelic drugs, and this might help the project. In one experiment, fans were sending an image of a man in the lotus position with his chakras, or energy centers, all brightly colored. Bessent dreamed about a man who was "suspended in midair or something" and "using natural energy." Remarkably, he reported seeing "the light from the sun...a spinal column."

SIGNS, STORIES, EXPERIMENTS, AND SYMBOLS

I dreamed that my mother's luggage was fashioned in the shape of a huge, pink poodle. I lifted it by the awkward woolly handle. "It's no good, they will never let us on the airplane with that ridiculous thing," I said as I looked down into its black beady eyes. "I will have to go and ask at the flight desk about this. Now, time is running short, so DO NOT move from this spot or we'll miss the plane to Italy."

I left my mother and my wife, Jane, standing outside the airport duty-free shop with its tempting bargains and hurried off with the bag to find a fight attendant. I think I'd made my point about not moving, but I knew it was like asking Dracula to wait besides a blood bank.

By the time I returned with the flight attendant, we were desperately late and would have to dash to catch the airplane. "Where's Mom?" I asked. "I don't know," replied Jane. "She's gone shopping, but I have no idea where she is now." There followed a period of frantic activity, announcements, and after a hopeless search for mother, I woke up.

I began to describe my dream to Jane, but she knew the plot for she'd had exactly the same dream except from a slightly different perspective. Jane dreamed of me arriving with the flight attendant and had spent her dream urging my mom not to go shopping while I was absent. Amazingly, the words spoken in her dream were exactly the same as in my dream and so were many other details, including the poodle bag. Apparently, Jane and I communicated in the dream. We had experienced dream telepathy.

The vacation went without a hitch, perhaps because we heeded the dreams' advice. And mother did not bring a poodle bag! The dream is of interest because it occurred on the same day that the contract arrived for this book. Maybe my unconscious was helping me by giving me an interesting example of a psychic dream.

Telepathy themes include dreaming of talking to the other dreamer on the **telephone** or communicating with them by **e-mail** or **letter**. Look to see if your dreams contain any other communication themes such as a carrier **pigeon**, a message on the **radio**, an unusual **advertisement**, or **graffiti** messages. Your dreams may be set in the same **city** or **country** and may feature similar people. Watch also for concurrent themes, emotions, and any other shared content. Dreams have a strange way of distorting things. For example, your friend may dream of eating, and you may dream of shopping for food. Similarly, dreams also speak in **puns**, so watch for the way your dreams play with words. For example, a telepathic message from a friend named Mike may result in you dreaming of a **microphone**; Tony, a **toe** or **knee**; and Barbara, a **bra** on **barbed wire**.

See also: **Extra Sensory Perception (ESP)**, **Mutual Dreams**

TIME

I never use an alarm clock. I can hardly wait until 5 A.M. In the army I always woke before reveille. I hate sleeping. It wastes time.

ISAAC ASIMOV, AUTHOR

Some scientists say that we dream continuously when sleeping; others claim that dreams occur only at certain times during the sleep cycle. However, we know that most vivid dreams occur during what psychologists call REM sleep. REM is short for rapid eye movements and is important because when people are dreaming, their eyes move rapidly from side to side under the lids. REM sleep is also known as paradoxical sleep or para-sleep. Watching a sleeping person's eyes move alerts psychologists to when a dream is taking place and has been a very useful key in helping to unlock the secrets of dreams. If you wake up a person during REM sleep, the person will usually claim to have been dreaming.

REM sleep tends to come in five episodes during the night. The episodes become longer and at shorter intervals as the night passes. Some of the most intense dreams occur just before you wake up, so setting the alarm clock a little earlier than normal will enable you to catch some of your most vivid dreams and also maybe a psychic dream or two.

Precognitive dreams usually occur between 3:00 A.M. and 7:00 A.M. when digestion has been completed and the mind and body are relaxed. In addition, 3:00 A.M. until 7:00 A.M. is a time when there are few external distractions, such as people moving around or traffic noise. Dreams in the early part of the night are more likely to be influenced by the events of the day and things you may have read or seen on TV before going to bed. Indigestion can also cause nightmares and strange dreams because the subconscious will turn bodily discomforts into symbols. For example, if you have constipation or a runny nose, you may dream of blocked tunnels.

Did you know that you spend nearly one-third of your life sleeping? If you sleep an average of 8 hours a day, by the age of 80 you will have slept 233,600 hours, or 26.67 years! You also dream 4 to 5 times a night and will have had 116,800 to 146,000 dreams by the age of 80. You spend about 6 years of your life dreaming.

Despite the regularity of the dream cycle, time in dreams behaves in very strange ways. Have you noticed that during dreams the past, present, and future may become muddled? You may, for example, have a dream of being a child; yet at the same time, the dream features people you only know in adulthood. Sometimes, distant events are recalled so clearly, it is as if they happened only yesterday. Dreams seem to have a wanton disregard for the idea that time travels in a straight line. They can put you in touch with a timeless quality in which events from the past or future are as real as events happening to you now.

It is no wonder that many people believe that dreams take them into another time and space. One of the most influential popular writers to address this subject was

J.W. Dunne, who proposed that in sleep we perceive different times. His book, *An Experiment with Time*, was written in 1911 when conventional wisdom regarding time was that all reality is confined to the instant called "now." He felt that the past and the future are purely imaginary. Albert Einstein had written his first paper on relativity in 1905, and Dunne was influenced by Einstein's new ideas. Dunne claimed that events could be observed as occupying space, spread out so that parts of the past and future were accessible during dreams. Dunne also quoted H.G. Wells' *The Time Machine* in support of his ideas. However, Wells replied that Dunne had taken his concept of "duration as a dimension of space" too seriously. Nonetheless, Dunne was an important pioneer of psychic dreaming and is certainly responsible for popularizing the subject.

SIGNS, STORIES, EXPERIMENTS, AND SYMBOLS

Time is often important in a dream when your life is under pressure. It is common to dream about missing trains, being late for work, or hurrying to catch a **bus**. These dreams express your anxieties about not being able to cope with your commitments. Certain times shown in a dream may also symbolize specific worries. For example, one minute to **midnight** implies a pensive situation and the possibility that things are going to change dramatically. This dream may express your worries but could also be a glimpse of future events. You may associate **noon** with lunch and nourishment, and you may connect 5:00 P.M. with finishing work. Again, these usually symbolize emotional conditions, but they may also indicate forthcoming events.

It is likely that dreams about the future will include symbols of the future, such as **clocks**, **sundials**, burning **candles**, **standing stones**, ancient **pyramids**, and even a **time machine**. When these symbols appear in a dream, they may be an indication that this dream is prophetic. The other content of the dream may represent the specific nature of potential opportunities and pitfalls for the future.

Superstition says that to dream about a **clock** denotes danger from an enemy. If it chimes, you will have unpleasant news, possibly news about a death. A burning **candle** shows that you can trust your friends, but if it is snuffed out, your friends are in serious trouble. If an unmarried woman dreams of candles, she will have a secret lover.

One of the oldest Western symbols of time is the **serpent** Ouroboros, the tail devourer. This symbolizes completion, perfection, and totality, as well as the endless round of existence and eternity. It is usually represented as a worm or serpent with its tail in its mouth. It was thought of as a fortunate omen if it appeared in a dream. Chinese fishermen and people living along the coast of China talk of the *Meng-chong* or "**Dream Worm**" that is said to travel between dreams and people, bringing insight into each others' past and future wrongdoings.

In 1865, August Kekule, a chemist, made an important discovery when he dreamed of a snake biting its tail in 1865. Up until that time, molecular structures were conceived of as being linear. The dream revealed to Kekule that many of benzene's unexplained properties could be understood if the molecules formed a ring.

See also: **Serialism**

TRIBAL DREAM INTERPRETATION

A long time ago, my father told me what his father had told him, that there was once a Lakota holy man, called "Drinks Water," who dreamed what was to be... He dreamed that the four-leggeds were going back to the Earth and that a strange race would weave a web all around the Lakotas. He said, "You shall live in square gray houses in a barren land..." Sometimes dreams are wiser than waking.

BLACK ELK, NATIVE AMERICAN HOLY MAN

Tribal societies believed that the soul detached from the body in sleep and would travel to different places. (The ancient Egyptians and Chinese believed this as well.) Tribes in New Guinea believed that if a dreamer saw a neighboring village preparing for battle, the whole tribe would take the dream seriously and immediately prepare for war. Similar beliefs hold true for the natives of Greenland and America. What happens in a dream is considered to have happened to the soul. For many African tribes, the dream life is held in such high regard, it is believed that dream battles can take place. If a man wakes with an aching limb, he will assume that he has been fighting his enemies. During sleep the soul is vulnerable, and many superstitions relate to protecting a sleeping person. Native Americans would paint the face of a sleeping enemy so the returning soul would not recognize its body and would be lost.

Tribal people believed that dreams were completely real and that the laws of waking life had to be applied to what happened in a dream and the dreamer punished accordingly. For example, if you dreamed of sleeping with another person's partner and you confessed to having dreamed this, you would be punished by the counsel of elders as if you had committed the act in real life. Centuries before Freud, tribes such as the Iroquois considered dreams to be the language of the soul that spoke from the dreamer's most secret wishes and was therefore considered to be truer than everyday language. Even the intent shown in a dream was punishable. There is an interesting recorded case in which a Native American dreamed that a missionary had stolen his pumpkin seeds. He demanded compensation even though the seeds were still in his possession and the missionary was 200 miles away when the dream occurred. He claimed that the missionary would have stolen the seed if he had been there.

Dreams were so important in some tribal societies, few dared question their validity. The Senoi people from the jungles of the central highlands of Malaysia believed that the characters in a dream could help a person conduct everyday life. Studies of the Senoi made by the anthropologist Kilton Stewart in the 1930s showed that they told and analyzed their dreams every morning. Children, especially, were advised to live according to what their dreams told them to do. Tribal man believed in his dreams more than he did his reason or what his senses told him. He counted on his dreams to guide his affairs in ways we would consider preposterous. For instance, if a primitive person dreamed he owned someone else's property and told the owner, the owner would willingly give him possession of the property without any resistance.

In many tribes, dreams were told either to the elders or to the medicine man. You would be asked to explain the dream to the shaman and together would discover its meaning. In particular, you would be expected to act on whatever it told you to do. Often the dreams were considered to be sent from the gods. In the case of the Zulu people, they were regarded as messages from the ancestors.

In tribal societies, the shaman was the magician, medium, medicine man, or healer. He owed his powers to mystical communication with the spirit world. Shamans are found among the Siberians, Eskimos, Lapps, Native American tribes, and in Southeast Asia and Oceania. In some tribal societies, the shaman does the dreaming for the whole tribe.

Many people today are embracing these archaic beliefs and practicing shamanic techniques. We see the symbolism of the shaman in movies like *The Matrix*, where the hero Neo (Keanu Reeves) explores dreamlike worlds for the benefit of others and in the hope of discovering the true reality. Modern shamans, just like their ancient counterparts, use autohypnotic trances to connect with the spirit world and experience ecstatic states of being and heightened perceptions. Most shamans in traditional tribal societies are men, but some shamans are women and are referred to as *brujas*, *curanderas*, or medicine women.

Dreams play a very important role in traditional shamanic sorcery. In dreams, a shaman may explore the astral worlds and call on spirit helpers or seek out totem power animals to aid in the spiritual work of the tribe. In particular, the old traditions used methods of working with lucid dreams in which the dreamer becomes conscious of the dream while it is taking place. The technique is used to travel out of the body and move beyond the physical body. These journeys of soul may take the shaman into the nether realms, higher levels of existence, parallel dimensions, or other regions of this world. Some people claim that these dreams of flight are real experiences.

Recent medical research, particularly with people who have come close to death during surgery, has presented science with considerable evidence to suggest that our awareness can travel outside the body at times of illness, crisis, and during sleep.

Native Americans have always regarded dreams as tremendously important and of great benefit to the education of the young. Children with rich dream lives were initiated into the dream traditions from an early age and were trained to become the future wise men of the tribes. In particular, Native Americans have a great insight into psychic dreams and how they connect us with other worlds and the afterlife. For example, the Iroquois of the Great Lakes used dreams to dictate their choices about fishing, hunting, war, dancing, and marriage. In particular, they paid attention to dreams their people had prior to war and hunting. If a tribe member's dream included a prophecy of failure, a hunting or war party would turn back.

Vivid dreamers such as Black Elk, of the Sioux tribe, have recorded the story of their life. Their fascinating writings show that dreams were hugely important in these societies. Dreams and waking visions were interwoven into the fabric of Native American society, where men of the tribe undertook dream quests as part of their initiation. This ritual would awaken their ability to have guiding visions and dreams.

Many tribes believed that a dream would come true if you acted it out in real life. They devised special methods of interpretation to understand psychic dreams. These methods included recording all the thoughts connected with the dream to establish a picture of what it represented. Once the meaning was understood, the community would "make it come true" in reality or through enactment and role-playing. In the 1860's a dream about paradise by a Paiute named Wodziwob inspired the famous ghost dances, with the intent of making his utopian vision a reality. A similar dream vision by Wovoka in 1889 triggered a frenzy of circle dancing across the Indian nation in the vain hope of regaining their lands and the burial sites of their ancestors.

Some Native American beliefs about dreams were a prelude to our modern theories. Freud believed that our hidden desires are revealed in dreams. The Huron tribe believed that the "voice" of the Great Spirit gave cryptic messages in dreams and revealed the hidden wishes of the soul. They believed that expressing its desires in dreams might satisfy the soul. Freud of course showed how repressed sexual passion may express itself in dreams. Similarly, Freud's discoveries about psychosomatic illness reflect many traditional Native American beliefs. The Huron under-stood that health is only achieved when the "spirit" inside us is made happy by expressing its desires in dream form. Certainly, the theo-ries of psychologist Carl Jung were directly influenced by his meetings in 1925 with Ochwiay Biano, the chief of the Taos Pueblo tribe of New Mexico. The chief explained to Jung that the whites were "mad" and unhappy in their relentless desires, and the cause of the malady lay in the fact that they could only think with their head and not with their heart. These ideas had a profound influence on Jung and helped to shape his theories.

Many Native Americans believe that dreams are like spirits that visit us while we sleep. Today, many modern Americans hang dream catchers by their beds. Invented by members of the Ojibwa tribe, these were originally used to protect children from nightmares. When dreams traveled through the web paths, the bad dreams lost their way and were entangled, disappearing with the first rays of daybreak. The good dreams, knowing the way, passed through the center and were guided gently to the sleeping person.

Could it be that psychic dreaming has been with us since Stone Age times? The answer may lie with the Australian Aboriginal culture, which dates back over 65,000 years and with their fascinating dream traditions that continue to this day. In particular, the Aboriginal "Dreamtime" is the foundation of their culture. It represents time of the creation of the world in Australian Aboriginal mythology and explains the origins of the land and its people. The Aboriginal people believe that they may leave their body and temporarily enter Dreamtime during sleep, connecting with ancient times of creation. They believe also that every living thing has a life essence called *kurunba*, which is renewed by connecting with the Dreamtime, and particularly when traveling along the old path-ways crossing the outback. While connected to these energies, spirits from underground rise and wander in the land of the living, passing through "clever men" (shaman) and giving them extra sensory powers. Young initiates will plug straight into this spiritual network and know their way around the wilderness and the locations of waterholes and magical and sacred places without any prior knowledge or experience of the outback.

The Aborigines feel that their ancestors walk with them and are present during dreaming. In dreams, dead relatives communi-cate and may bring healing if the dreamer is ill. Their ancestors also establish a link with the tribe as it journeys across the outback. During this time, they may appear as an actual visionary person. When their work is done, they change into animals, stars, hills, or other landmarks. For the Aborigines, therefore, the landscape is an externalization of their inner world and a symbol of their culture and heritage.

The experience of dreaming and Dreamtime connects the Aborigines with the oneness of nature and creation. This inner harmony brings with it many psychic powers. For example, Aborigines will know if a distant relative is troubled or in danger. There are cases recorded by the Australian anthropologist A. P. Elkin where the Aborigine will announce with complete certainty that a loved one at a distance is ill, dying, or in childbirth. Cases are recorded where distant family members with greater vision were prompted to hurry to them. Using their surprisingly intuitive knowledge of herbal medicine, Aborigines would bring with them the herbs needed to treat the ailing family member.

SIGNS, STORIES, EXPERIMENTS, AND SYMBOLS

According to the Aborigines, every meaningful activity and event leaves behind a vibration in the land itself. Even the shape of the landscape tells of the time of creation and the gods that made the world. The Aborigines call this resonance the "Dreaming" of a place. For them, this is a sacred energy. Only when a person is in an extraordinary state of consciousness can that person become aware of this inner Dreaming of the earth. Aboriginal art reflects these ideas and in it are many levels of meaning that remain obscure to the uninitiated observer. When an Aborigine is in touch with these non-ordinary levels of reality, they call it "using the strong eye" and believe that it puts them in touch with other people and also other species. Associated with these powers are many special magical places, rocks, art, and symbols that to this day many Aborigines keep as closely guarded secrets.

The powers of the Aborigine shaman are considered by many to be more than fantasy but are an actualization of real psychic energy. In particular the entities described as "power animals" can sometimes be seen by others. Native Americans believe that human and animal spirits can interact with us in waking life and dreams to provide us with helpful information. For example, author Tony Crisp quotes a medicine man who made his discoveries via dreams. The medicine man said, "I saw **a dog** that had been shot through the neck and kidneys. I felt sorry for the dog and carried him home and took care of him. I slept with the dog beside me. While there, I had a bad dream. The dream changed, and the dog became a man. It spoke to me and said, 'Now, I will give you some roots for medicine and show you how to use them. Whenever you see someone who is ill and feel sorry for him, use this medicine, and he will be well.' One of these medicines is good for sore throat."

Could it be that modern-day dreamers who have realized inventions, creations, and discoveries by way of dreams are following in the footsteps of an ancient intuitive tradition that still resonates in tribal societies? Perhaps we, too, should listen to the advice given by chief Ochwiay Biano to Carl Jung; we would gain great benefit if we could learn to think with the heart as well as the head.

·

See also: **Animal Psychics, Animal Spirits, Animal Symbols**

UNIDENTIFIED FLYING OBJECTS (UFOs)

I don't laugh at people any more when they say they've seen UFOs. It was the darndest thing I've ever seen. It was big, it was very bright, it changed colors, and it was about the size of the moon. We watched it for 10 minutes, but none of us could figure out what it was.

JIMMY CARTER, FORMER PRESIDENT OF THE UNITED STATES

Some people argue that dreams and reports about UFOs are an exclusively modern phenomenon. They feel that UFOs are a symbolic reflection of the worries and concerns of modern people living in an uncertain world. Yet, many cultures tell of dreams and maintain ritual traditions that could be described as a history of contact with aliens. For example, in the Aboriginal culture, the shamans speak of meeting with the sky gods Baiame, Biral, Goin, and Bundjil during dreaming. These meetings are strikingly similar to recent reports made by people who claim to have been contacted or **abducted**.

In some instances, the dreamer is abducted by "spirits," ritualistically "killed," and then experiences a magical journey. This is generally described as an aerial ascent to a strange realm where the person is met by the "**sky god**." After his ordeal, he is restored to life in a transformed state and becomes fully initiated by the tribal shaman.

Many tribal traditions describe similar dreams, myths, and experiences about abduction by powerful beings. Sometimes, these abductions detail medical experimentation similar to the ones that **aliens** are supposed to have performed on today's abductees. These traditions and rituals involve symbolically removing body parts, disemboweling the abductee, implanting artifacts, and ascending to the skies to visit strange lands.

Seventy percent of abductees begin their adventure in a dreamlike state. The abduction may occur in the person's bedroom or when he or she is driving at night. Could it be that these abductions are the result of lucid dreams? I have explained in the section on lucid dreams that they occur in a state of consciousness somewhere between sleep and waking. The person is asleep, but at the same time the mind is consciously active. Lucid dreams appear to the person to be a completely real experience with a full sense of space and time and with all five senses appearing to function as normal. This profoundly altered state of consciousness can easily be mistaken for a real experience and may occur in everyday situations when the person is close to a sleep state. Memories of these states can be remembered or recovered under hypnosis.

According to the research of psychologist Keith Ring and others, abductees as a group have suffered a higher than average incidence of child abuse. Children suffering abuse tend to develop a psychological defense mechanism that Freud called "dissociation." Freud believed they divide their awareness so that they can escape from the appalling physical realities. Because many abduction reports involve sexual experiments by the aliens, some people insist that this is actually childhood memory breaking through into normal consciousness. The space visitors' experiments are, in fact, a disguised fantasy about what happened to the person during childhood. These hidden memories can be mistaken for real events.

Encountering a UFO in a dream may suggest a longing for divine awareness.

SIGNS, STORIES, EXPERIMENTS, AND SYMBOLS

Carl Jung presented an interesting perspective on the UFO phenomenon in his book, *Flying Saucers: A Modern Myth of Things Seen in the Skies* (1958). According to Jung, the human psyche is struggling to reconcile the opposite aspects of itself and find inner harmony. The battle of psychological opposites includes the conflict between the extroverted, or outgoing, side of yourself and the introverted, or inward looking, side of yourself. There are also conflicts between the integrated conscious and unconscious self, or God-image; the persona, or social mask, versus the shadow, or unconscious natural self; and thinking and feeling, or rational functions, versus sensation and intuition, or irrational forces. These opposites are brought together by healing symbols from the collective unconscious that Jung called the archetypes. One of the oldest and most powerful archetypal symbols is the mandala. This comes from the Sanskrit word meaning **"magic circle"** and is a symbol for the fully integrated and whole self. Jung argued that the circular nature of UFOs, or flying saucers, is a symbolic representation of man's desire to find the wholeness of self that this mandala represents. Crop circles may be a similar symbol of people's hope for wholeness. What our culture calls abductions may be distorted views of the search for the true self to discover the fullness of the human psyche.

If you dream about **aliens** and UFOs, it does not necessarily mean that you are about to be abducted or whisked off to another planet. These dreams are more likely to be about your own journey of self-discovery and your desire to understand more about the unfamiliar part of your psyche.

If your dream is frightening, it may indicate that you consider this unknown part of yourself hostile. If this is the case, you need to find out why you consider this part of yourself an enemy. The appearance of an alien in a dream may represent part of yourself that you consider alien to your normal nature. You may be having feelings that are "unlike you" or not in keeping with your normal ways of behaving. It could be that you have repressed some of your feelings and emotions. Now, these things press on you during sleep. Is there a problem that you do not want to face or an issue that requires your attention? Perhaps you feel alienated socially or at the workplace. You may feel that your views are so different from everyone else's that you may as well come from another planet.

If the alien speaks wisdom to you, maybe this is your own higher self connecting with you. Perhaps this innate wisdom also gives you an overview of a situation and even an insight into the future along with insight on how to deal with it. The higher functions of the intuition will often appear in a symbolic form such as a **wise man** or **wise woman**, a **sage**, **alchemist**, **guru**, **witch**, or **wizard**. Because it comes from the skies, the alien can represent the search for the divine. Perhaps this dream holds clues to discovering your true nature and the way to divine awareness. Listen to the messages the alien brings. Good or bad, the dream may give you some unusual and helpful insights from your unconscious.

UNCONSCIOUS MIND

*Everything of which I know, but of which I am
not at the moment thinking; everything of which
I was once conscious but have now forgotten;
everything perceived by my senses, but not
noted by my conscious mind; everything which,
involuntarily and without paying attention
to it, I feel, think, remember, want, and do;
all the future things that are taking shape in
me and will sometime come to consciousness:
all this is the content of the unconscious.*

CARL JUNG, SWISS PSYCHOLOGIST

Freud believed that the unconscious stores repressed memories. These are experiences that are too painful to remember, so the mind pushes them into the darkness. These painful hidden memories can manifest in dreams, and if they are not dealt with they can result in neurotic or psychotic behavior. Jung extended this theory and claimed that the unconscious isa reservoir of transcendent truths. He spoke of the "personal unconscious" that contains the memories which were conscious at one time but which have now disappeared and been forgotten or repressed. However, Jung also speaks of the "collective unconscious," which contains memories that have not been individually acquired.

Jung claimed that people not only have their own personal unconscious mind, but also share some elements of their nature with all other people. He called this shared unconscious the collective unconscious. The material from the collective unconscious touches themes and symbols that are common to all people. Jung called these the archetypes. He proposed that archetypes, or images and memories of important human experiences, are passed down through the generations. These archetypes can be common designs, shapes, colors, and figures seen throughout time in the mythology and religions of cultures all over the world.

In a lecture, Jung said, "There exists a second psychic system of a collective, universal, and impersonal nature which is identical in all individuals. This collective unconscious does not develop individually, but is inherited. It consists of pre-existent forms, the archetypes, which can only become conscious secondarily and which give definite form to certain psychic contents."

SIGNS, STORIES, EXPERIMENTS, AND SYMBOLS

One of Jung's most important messages to us is that the purpose of human life is to become conscious. "As far as we can discern," he writes, "the sole purpose of human existence is to kindle a light in the darkness of mere being."

One way of doing this is to explore the unconscious through your dreams. Your dreams can help you to become aware of your hidden potential, motives, and fears. When brought into the light of consciousness, you can integrate unconscious content into your personality enabling you to grow spiritually and to achieve a balance between mind and body, spirit and instinct.

UNIVERSAL MIND

*I do not believe that I am dreaming, but I
cannot prove that I am not.*

BERTRAND RUSSELL, BRITISH MATHEMATICIAN
AND PHILOSOPHER

The senses work by receiving information from an exterior source. For example, light enters the eyes, sound comes to the ears, airborne chemicals trigger smell, taste results from contact with a material, and touch is activated by pressure to the skin. Parapsychologists assume that ESP is a sixth sense and comes from an external source. This fits snugly into the scientific model of an objective and measurable material world. Our sixth sense is simply another way of interacting with and gaining information about the world. It can be explained within science's existing model of reality.

An alternative theory is that ESP psychic dreams come when you connect to what mystics have called the universal mind. This is the collective intelligence of the universe, the ultimate and totally inclusive supernormal intellect. Human consciousness is networked into this collective consciousness, meaning that all your thoughts and experiences are connected to everyone else's thoughts and experiences. Therefore, ESP does not come to you like a signal from outside; it comes from within when you connect to that part of your nature that is linked to the universal mind. During periods of deep meditation or in the relaxed states of sleep and dreaming, you may become aware of your connection to this extraordinary state of being.

To discover your psychic powers, you need only look within yourself. For example, if I want to "remote view" another location, I do not need to leave my body. I simply look within and look for the part of me that is connected to that place. Similarly, telepathy occurs when you connect with another through this state of being. Time, too, is part of this universal mind; by looking within, you can connect to the record of all things that have ever happened or glimpse the potential future.

Some mystics believe that the universal mind exists on a subatomic level. Already there are microelectronic devices being designed that will function by using the spin of the electron (spintronics). Scientists believe that these devices will lead to quantum microchips. So, would it be a big surprise if we discovered that the mind penetrates the subcellular level and is directly plugged into the quantum world?

Quantum mechanics shows that there is no such thing as an emptiness, or nothingness, and that the void of space is buzzing with subatomic activity called zero-point energy. Quantum physics predicts the existence of an underlying sea of zero-point energy at every point in the universe. Could it be that quantum physics is describing what the Buddha called Nirvana, the Hindus called Brahma, and mystics call the sea of light? This universal mind connects everything together, including human consciousness. ESP may occur when our intuition touches these quantum levels where "here" and "there" are one and the same.

SIGNS, STORIES, EXPERIMENTS, AND SYMBOLS

If ESP were a type of radio signal, you would assume that it would get weaker over a distance. However, this does not appear to be the case. The power of telepathy works over vast distances. One of the most interesting experiments with telepathy was undertaken by Edgar Mitchell from the command module of *Apollo 14*. He attempted to link up with six colleagues tuning in 250,000 miles away on earth. Mitchell transmitted images of J.B. Rhine's Zener cards, showing the symbols of a square, circle, cross, star, and wavy lines. Unfortunately, he was only able to complete four of the six experiments. The data indicated that there was only a 1 in 3,000 probability that the results were due to chance.

The experiment shows that distance is not a hindrance. In fact, we may not be sending signals to one another at all but somehow connecting to the universal mind.

When Edgar Mitchell did his experiments, he described an overwhelming feeling of connectedness with all things. He was separated from humanity, yet at the same time he felt a compelling kinship. This is what the mystics have called the "ecstasy of unity" or the "oneness." Many of us have experienced this feeling of the resonance of all things during meditation or on waking from an extraordinary psychic dream. The theory of the universal mind lies at the heart of modern metaphysical teachings.

See also: **Synchronicity**

WICCA AND WITCHCRAFT

The monkey explores moon-in-water,
not resting, nor giving up, unto death.
Let go and disappear into the deep water,
the world will shine dazzling pure.

ZEN KOAN

Witchcraft and paganism are more popular than ever, and many people are now turning to pre-Christian religions for ancient knowledge and direct spiritual insight. Modern witchcraft is mainly based around a form developed in the Nineteenth century called Wicca, meaning "wise ones." Wiccans are usually members of a coven, or group, that is lead by a High Priestess and High Priest.

Wicca is inspired by the old nature religions that worshiped the Earth and the seasons. It places great importance on the equinoxes and phases of the moon and celebrates the pre-Christian festivals of Yule, Imbolc, Lady Day, Beltaine, Midsummer, Lughnassad, Mabon, and Samhain. Wiccans believe that each natural cycle has its use in magic, and by living in tune with these natural phases you become more spiritually powerful and able to smooth your life's path.

Wiccans believe that psychic dreams are connected to nature's cycles. The seasons from spring to autumn are said to be periods of accelerated learning when you will receive teaching dreams about your life and path. The winter is understood to be the time when dreams are most vivid because this season is one of inner growth. During the winter, your dreams will assimilate the lessons from the previous seasons. It is the right time to seed your hopes for the future, using dream incubation, and to plan your goals for the coming spring.

Dreams enhance the practitioner's supernatural powers and assist the actualization of a ritual's powers. In particular, the sleeper learns to control his or her magical powers when dreaming and to use dreams as a means to directly influence people and events. Some forms of sorcery encourage the dreamer to awaken in the dream and to perform dream actions, such as bringing the hands together during a dream. These techniques trigger lucid dreaming and give the practitioner access to special powers that may include the ability to appear in other people's dreams. Some of the stories of flying witches probably originate from descriptions of lucid dreams or similar states of consciousness triggered by hallucinogenic potions. Lucid dreaming may enable the practitioner to enter altered states of consciousness and access other realities.

Of particular importance to the followers of magic is the influence of the **moon**. For

In Wicca and Witchcraft, a dream is regarded as a source of prophecy and magical power.

the Wiccan, the moon is a real force that has a powerful effect on your inner state. It has long been known that the gravity of the moon affects life on Earth, and ancient pagans used to harness her powers for insight into the future, for spiritual healing, and as a force for good. For example, you may work a spell at an auspicious lunar cycle and then dream that evening about your wish coming true. It is said that if this happens, it will not be long until the dream becomes a reality.

According to Wiccan lore, the content and quality of dreams can be affected by the lunar cycle. Five days before a full moon, dreams are said to become more vivid and gradually to reach complete lucidity as the moon becomes full. If you are not at peace with yourself, the full moon can disrupt your psychic energy, and your dreams may be frightening or strange. The term "lunatic" is based on the fact that asylum inmates were often disturbed at the time of a full moon. Some people may become depressed or experience mood swings and exhaustion during a full moon cycle. However, if you are centered and in control of your own life, this time can be one of great spiritual progress, using the moon's energy to your advantage.

The moon is associated with the power of the goddess and her powers of intuition, clairvoyance, and dream insight. Moon magic is personified by three goddesses that are aligned to the three main phases of the moon:

Maiden: The moon is waxing. This is a time when dreams may inspire you with new ideas.

Mother: The moon is full. This is a time of great lucidity and healing when magical powers can be used.

Crone: The moon is waning. The crone or matriarch gives wisdom and insight into the future.

SIGNS, STORIES, EXPERIMENTS, AND SYMBOLS

The Wiccans' beloved moon may also represent your own inner state. Carl Jung explained that when a **circle** appears in a dream, it is a sign that the person is moving toward psychological wholeness. A full **moon** may, therefore, represent the totality of the self and higher consciousness. If the moon is eclipsed, it shows that something in the personality is being repressed. Freud would say that this shows that you are getting rid of the attachment to your **mother**. In earlier times, eclipses were considered to be a prelude to disaster. If your dream is prophetic, it may indicate worrying events on the horizon.

Within dreams, the moon can symbolize the possibility of personal growth. Associated with the goddess, the moon can also represent the feminine aspect of the self and anything hidden or mysterious.

In earlier times, when paganism and gnosticism were suppressed by the Church, witchcraft themes in dreams were considered to be very bad omens as they were associated with the **devil** and all his works. They boded ill for love and business ventures. In some superstitions the symbolism is reversed, and a **witch,** for example, forecasts a time of hilarious enjoyment. Similarly, in some dream books a **wizard** is thought to predict you will have a big family but also a broken engagement. Dreams about the **devil** may bring despair and failure. If a farmer dreams of the devil, it indicates that crops will fail. This is a particularly odd superstition because the form of the devil was based on the cloven-footed god **Pan**, who brought fertility and abundance to the people of the ancient world.

The symbols associated with witchcraft will also appear in dreams as images that represent what's happening in your own psychology. A **witch**, for instance, may represent a destructive aspect of the unconscious. She may symbolize something that you have repressed and that is trying to get recognition. She may represent negative qualities, such as moodiness, dislike of women, deceit, or jealousy. A **wizard** may encapsulate qualities of egotism and misuse of power. If the **devil** appears in your dream, he probably symbolizes the things about yourself that you fear, in particular, repressed sexual desires. As he comes from the underground world, he may represent things from the unconscious that lie "below" normal awareness. He is a symbol that includes all your hidden fears.

See also: **Dream Incubation (Seeding), Lucid Dreams, Telepathy**

WORK

You know, I would rather have been a professional golfer, but my family pushed me into politics.

DAN QUAYLE, FORMER VICE PRESIDENT OF THE UNITED STATES

Are you dreaming of a better career? Psychic dreams may show you the way to career success by highlighting your feelings and exposing potential opportunities and pitfalls in your future. When I ran my own advertising/design agency, my dreams would often alert me to new business opportunities. Sometimes, the dreams would identify new clients. On one occasion, a dream even supplied me with a potential customer's name. He called the next day. Clearly, psychic dreams can prove very helpful if you want to make progress in your career.

ESP may often happen to you at work. For example, if you are sensitive to telepathic signals, you may become aware of the people in the office who are plotting against you. You may feel their negative energy and take steps to counter any actions they may take. If you are not sure about the situation, your dreams may alert you to the nature of the problem. You may dream of **betrayal** or being **stabbed** in the back. The reverse may be true for those you get along with at work. You may anticipate each other's telephone calls or e-mails before they arrive and may share a feeling of good energy when you meet.

Dreams may also make you aware of other activities happening at work about which the staff has no knowledge. A hostile takeover by another business may be highlighted in your dreams or your dreams may reveal plans to lay off some employees. Because dreams speak in the language of symbols, you will need to study your dreams to understand what secrets are being shown to you. For example, a warning of a takeover may be represented by a big fish eating a smaller fish or perhaps by a demolition crew arriving at your workplace. In addition, the possibility of being fired may be represented in dreams about being abandoned. You may dream of someone you love letting you down or of being shipwrecked. There are millions of ways a dream can use symbolism to express your situation and feelings. With practice, you will begin to see how the symbols being used in the dream express things about your situation and the potential future.

Trusting your dream intuition will help you get sales leads, foresee opportunities, and protect you from the hazards of career changes by giving you insights into the potential future. They may also highlight your anxieties about work and suggest ways that you can gain success and security.

In February 2003, I was commissioned by a public relations consultant to help promote the British government's incentive called "Learn Direct." This campaign encouraged people to learn new work skills by entering training programs. My job was to see if people were having nightmares about work and to see if these were connected to anxieties about their skills. To do this, we set up a sample survey of 1,000 adults.

Our dream survey revealed some interesting facts that may show that longer working hours and additional job pressures are penetrating the subconscious: 57 percent of adults admitted to suffering from nightmares about their jobs. Stress in the workplace was revealed as the chief cause of dread dreams, with 51 percent citing this as contributing to their nightmares. Nearly 25 percent of these nightmares took place on a Sunday night, giving rise to "Sunday night syndrome," as the nation's subconscious manifests its dread of the impending week.

At the top of the list of our work-related themes were dreams about arguing with the boss; dreams about killing the boss were at number eight on our list. Other dreams that show vulnerability and anxieties included being late, having to do an unexpected presentation, going to work naked, computers crashing, and getting sacked.

Clearly, psychic and spiritual dreams are going to be pushed to the back burner for many people if their subconscious is preoccupied with work. You will know you are on the spiritual path when these anxiety dreams lessen and your dreams have time to delve into the mysteries of existence and the wonders of the unconscious. Obviously, many people need to get their priorities straight if they are ever going to find the inner peace that is the perennial promise of spirituality.

WORLD EVENTS

I never make predictions.
I never have, and I never will.

TONY BLAIR, BRITISH PRIME MINISTER

When people dream of cataclysmic world events, they wonder whether their dreams may be about the future. Vivid dreams of crashes, explosions, terrorist attacks, and assassinations do sometimes come true. In my news columns, I have included many examples of people who claim to have foreseen the death of Princess Diana, the Chernobyl nuclear tragedy, or the 9/11 attacks. Similarly, there are a number of documented cases from people who claimed to have dreamed of the assassination of President Kennedy. However, remember that we all dream several dreams every night and, considering the huge population of the Western world and JFK's world fame, it is likely that someone somewhere would have dreamed of his killing.

So, we have to be a little careful when we make claims of foreseeing world events. I have met psychics who make such long lists of predictions that the odds are high that some of them will come true. When this

Vivid dreams of world events (such as the Earth being hit by an asteroid) can signify real dangers.

happens, they make a big fuss about the ones they got right, but they completely ignore the ones that were off target. If you are honest with yourself, you need to keep a careful record of your dreams that come true, but you also must take into account the dream predictions that don't come true. In this way, you can arrive at a fair assessment about your ability to have precognitive dreams.

On occasion, dreams may appear that are so precise in their detail that the odds of this being a coincidence are astronomical. If you continue to have highly accurate dreams about world events, this may suggest that you have a true paranormal insight.

SIGNS, STORIES, EXPERIMENTS, AND SYMBOLS

If you believe that you have had a dream about upcoming world events, you should try to verify the information in the dream. There is a psychic in Great Britain who draws pictures of his dreams about world events and takes them with him to his local bank. There, he stands in front of the date clock and has a photograph taken of him holding the picture. In this way, he is able to prove the date of the drawing.

Psychic dreamers have used the message boards on my Web site to post their premonitions and psychic dream insights. A visitor with the user name Yaqiatee posted one interesting example. My site helper and fellow medium, Vi Kipling, reported the story on our news pages and later interviewed the visitor.

On May 17, 2002, Yaqiatee put the following prediction on the Premonitions Board: "I wonder if anyone else has felt or seen that June 14th might be a disaster day? While the symbolic reference would be Jewish and Moslem, with Jerusalem as a focus, the area of damage will be in the West. Originally, I thought it would be Jerusalem, but today I am not so sure. I saw the date in big green letters in my mind about four or five weeks ago as I was driving, and it so happens I was thinking about the conflict in the Middle East. My own context of the date is horrific....Sorry. I hope I am wrong....I will try to open this path if I can...."

Many site visitors added their thoughts and feelings about this particular day, and soon there were a great many postings about the date. Nothing happened, and everyone felt a little foolish about getting so excited about the date. A site visitor posed the question, "So, what did happen on June 14th?"

A subsequent visitor to the Premonitions Board pointed out that on June 14th, the world was very nearly involved in a disaster of major proportions, which was not known or reported until June 17th. The information from the BBC Web site read:

"Astronomers have revealed that on June 14th, an asteroid the size of a football field made one of the closest ever recorded approaches to the Earth. It is only the sixth time an asteroid has been seen to penetrate the moon's orbit, and this is by far the biggest rock to do so. What has worried some astronomers, though, is that the space object was only detected on June 17th, several days after its flyby. It was found by astronomers working on the Lincoln Laboratory Near-Earth Asteroid Research (Linear) search program in New Mexico.

"Catalogued as 2002MN, the asteroid was traveling at over 23,000 miles per hour when it passed Earth at a distance of about 75,000 miles. The last time such an object was recorded to have come this close was in December 1994.

"The space rock has a diameter of between 160 and 320 feet. This is actually quite small when compared with many other asteroids and incapable of causing damage on a global scale. Nonetheless, an impact from such a body would still be dangerous. If 2002MN had hit the Earth, it would have caused local devastation similar to that which occurred in Tunguska, Siberia in 1908, when 772 square miles of forest were flattened.

"A major issue of concern centers on how late this object was picked up. Dr. John Davies of the Royal Observatory in Edinburgh, Scotland, has calculated the orbit of the asteroid from the Linear data. He concludes that the asteroid came out of the sun and was impossible for Linear to see until one hour after its flyby of the Earth on the 14th."

While it cannot be proved that this was the disaster Yaqiatee warned about, thankfully, the asteroid did not hit the earth. The report does not include a speculation as to where it is thought the asteroid would have hit the earth, but it is very interesting to note that the observatory which did eventually pick it up was in New Mexico.

Yaqiatee is a gentleman in his prime who lives in Alaska when not traveling the world for his job. Naturally, he was pleased, as we all were, that the asteroid did miss Earth. He felt comfortable with the thought that this "near miss" could account for his feelings of impending disaster on June 14th.

Sometimes, it is possible to be aware of an impending disaster or catastrophe that does not take place. Nothing in life is set in concrete, and the events which were shaping a future disaster could change, averting the disaster.

See also: **Accidents, Disasters**

XENOGLOSSY

Harken unto my voice.

JOHN DEE, BRITISH MATHEMATICIAN AND PHILOSOPHER

Xenoglossy means speaking or writing a language entirely unknown to the speaker. The phenomenon is frequently present in incidents of past-life recall and in states of altered consciousness, such as trance, delirium, and mediumship. Occasionally, an unknown and unlearned foreign language may be heard in dreams.

The jury is still out as to whether this is a real phenomenon or the result of forgotten phrases emerging from the subconscious. Many instances are clearly gibberish. Some researchers have claimed that the phenomenon is a result of telepathy between two people, such as hypnotist and subject. If this is true, it is astonishing that the telepathic "receiver" can not only "read" the words in the sender's mind but also put the individual words into sentences. This would be a truly formidable task.

I have encountered limited xenoglossy in my work as a medium. During mediumistic consultations, when I have been working with foreign sitters, I have occasionally spoken to them in their own language. This has included short sentences in Urdu, Croatian, and Chinese. I have no knowledge of any of these languages, but I was, of course, understood by the recipient. If a foreign language can be transmitted by spirits during mediumship, then could it not also happen in dreams or when under hypnosis?

Skeptics have pointed out that many instances of xenoglossy have been shown to be memories of words and phrases learned in the past but forgotten. However, there are rare instances when people have been able to spontaneously converse in an unlearned language. In 1961, Dr. Ian Stevenson and Professor Sri H.N. Banerjee documented one of the most famous cases. They were researching the alleged past-life recall of Swarnlata Mishra, a Hindu girl born in 1948. She claimed that she remembered her previous incarnation as a Bengali woman. A friend had taught her Bengali songs and dances during this past life. At the age of three in her present life, the young girl sang Bengali songs and performed Bengali dances without ever having been exposed to the Bengali language or culture.

SIGNS, STORIES, EXPERIMENTS, AND SYMBOLS

If you dream of **words** being spoken in a dream, you should write them down immediately on waking because auditory information is quickly forgotten. **Foreign languages** spoken in a dream can be symbolic of things you don't understand or that are unknown to you. Dreaming of **foreign countries** or **foreigners** may represent a part of the psyche that is unfamiliar to you. Such a dream may show that you are neglecting important feelings or talents. Foreign lands can symbolize the fact that you are experiencing something unusual in your waking life. The anxieties associated with a new relationship, new job, or strange experience may trigger these dreams.

In most instances, dreaming of foreign languages is symbolic of emotions and experiences that are perplexing to the dreamer. But what if on waking you were to write down sentences in a foreign language that you cannot speak but which translate into something intelligible? If this were the case,

you would have experienced xenoglossy and may have received information by clairvoyance. Interestingly, practitioners of the medieval "magick" of John Dee believe there is a special language of heaven called the "Enochian language" that is whispered to the sleeper by the **angels**. Dee claimed that Adam and Eve were the first people to speak the Enochian language, and many modern magicians believe it was the original language of Atlantis.

YOGA TRADITIONS

In deep meditation, the flow of concentration is continuous, like the flow of oil.

Patanjali, Indian author

Buddhism teaches that existence is an illusion. The true reality lies beyond duality and is only truly understood when the adept reaches the state of Nirvana. Everything else we experience in life is like an illusionary dream mirage. When Padmasambhava brought the teachings of the Buddha to Tibet over 1,300 years ago, he brought with him a tradition of tantric yoga that eventually formed an extraordinary symbiosis with the nature religion of Bon.'

An important aspect of Padmasambhava's teachings were the writings called *The Yoga of the Dream State*. These explained the practice of dream yoga and lucid dreaming, which he had learned in India from a yogi named Lawapa. The objective of these teachings is to realize the illusionary nature of existence and to free the practitioner from this illusion.

The Yoga of the Dream State teaches that dreams can be altered by the will and that they are unreal; they are like a fantasy or an illusion. This understanding can be brought

Dream yoga is a spiritual practice that opens the way to psychic skills and sacred states.

forward into normal waking consciousness so that the unreality of all existence can be recognized. Life is here today and gone tomorrow, and like a dream, it is transient and cannot be fixed in one spot. Dream yoga helps the Tibetan Buddhist see beyond the illusion and experience the oneness that hides behind the illusion of duality. Dreams can therefore be a useful aid in the quest of enlightenment.

The Tibetan system of dream yoga recognizes that some dreams deal with things that occur during the state of wakefulness. In addition, dreams can be received from the living or the dead. This system also believes that some dreams are symbolic and others contain portents of the future, omens, or warnings. The Tibetan system includes among the dream yoga techniques ESP dreams as well as "radiant dreams." The latter are super-lucid dreams that bring great spiritual teaching or blessing.

Tibetan dream yoga divides dreams into three categories:

Ordinary dreams: These are a result of the day's concerns or past experience and karma. These dreams are self-centered rather than spiritual; they are the ones that have been most studied by Western psychology.

Clear light dreams: These dreams have a transcendent quality and a feeling of the "I" as the observer being at one with the totality of the universal Self. They dreams may include awareness of spiritual teachings, visions, healing, and of the spiritual centers (chakras) in the aura. At the onset of clear light dreams you may see a kaleidoscope of colorful geometric shapes, which may become elastic and merge into one another. Some people also experience a hum or buzzing sound.

Lucid dreams: This is a dream in which you are aware you are dreaming while the dream is taking place. During lucid dreams, yogis can continue their spiritual practice by maintaining a state of awareness during sleep. It is a time when they will prepare themselves for liberation by becoming aware of their own mortality and the *bardo* states that lie beyond death. Some Tibetan adepts used these dreams to aquire special spiritual powers such as bilocation, telepathy, or for gaining control over their spiritual progress. When these states are mastered, sleep as we understand it is no longer necessary.

The Tibetans have developed elaborate techniques for inducing lucidity. Some of these are so esoteric, it is hard for the uninitiated Western mind to understand or practice. However, many of the recommended techniques are strikingly similar to the techniques now employed by Western lucid-dream researchers. For example, both use frequent reflection throughout the day on the dreamlike nature of reality.

In India, Patanjali, the author of the *Yoga Sutras*, writes that by mastery of the Yoga powers, a yogi acquires *siddhis* powers (magical powers) that give the adept direct knowledge of the past and the future. The purpose of yoga is to attain union with the Divine, and these powers are considered unimportant compared to the goal of enlightenment. In fact, psychic powers can be a distraction from the path to enlightenment if sought for their own sake or for selfish reasons. Nonetheless, it is interesting to note that psychic dreaming has been used as a spiritual practice for thousands of years and can, if used properly, benefit the development of your spirituality.

Eastern gurus point out that the *siddhis*

powers achieved in psychic dreaming and dream yoga have only limited use and that meditation and other spiritual practices are required to attain complete spiritual insight. You are, therefore, unlikely to become enlightened while sleeping. Nonetheless, you may gain some spiritual insights that will aid your inner development. The sages tell us that knowing that the body is sleeping and dreaming constitutes a special spiritual knowledge that goes beyond conscious thought. This state of being is hard to describe as it is a state of transcendence. It is said to release the practitioner of dream yoga from impurities and the obstacles of the mind. (In yoga, obstacles refer to the conditions that prevent our spiritual progress in both the inner and outer world.) By using dreams correctly, the mind of the practitioner of yoga-dreaming-methods becomes stable and ready to attain spiritual knowledge.

SIGNS, STORIES, EXPERIMENTS, AND SYMBOLS

During my late teens, I became very interested in yoga and, in particular, in the books by the guru Paramahansa Yogananda (1893-1952). He spent most of his life spreading spiritual knowledge in the United States. Some years later, I decided to learn about Yogananda's Kriya yoga methods, so I wrote to his organization, the Self-Realization Fellowship. In the space on the form that asked what my religion was, I wrote, "spiritualist." The reply from the organization was that Kriya yoga was not suitable for people who are interested in mediumship, and they returned my check.

Sadly, even in spiritual organizations, there is a lot of ignorance about the nature of mediumship. So, I decided to ask Yogananda myself, using dream yoga. As I prepared for sleep, I sent a thought out in the ether asking if I might be shown the yoga technique of Kriya yoga. That night, I dreamed of Yogananda. He said to me, "As you awaken, listen to your ears."

When I awoke, there was a ringing in my ears. I was to discover some time later that this is one of the most important techniques of Kriya yoga. The adept practitioner listens to the sounds of the inner ear and uses this to prepare for meditation, eventually fixing on the sound of the mantra "Om."

I believe that as long as you have sincere intent you can connect with great spiritual beings and learn from them through psychic dreams. In the East, people accept that if you don't meet the guru in life, he may connect to you through a dream. I have also had similar experiences with the living guru Sai Baba. I have been given specific guidance in a dream, and this guidance has proven to be the right course to take. I have also spoken with many people who have experienced similar dream instruction from Sai Baba, Vivekananda, Milarepa, Sri Aurobindo, Mother Meera, and other great beings. All we need do is ask.

See also: **Guides and Gurus, Lucid Dreams, Out-of-Body Experiences (OBEs)**

ZODIAC

Astrology, like the collective unconscious with which psychology is concerned, consists of symbolic configurations; the "planets" are the gods, symbols of the power of the unconscious.

CARL JUNG, SWISS PSYCHOLOGIST

Carl Jung made use of astrology in his practice of psychotherapy. When he came to an impasse with a difficult patient, he would have the birth chart of the person drawn up and would interpret it from a psychological standpoint. Jung was particularly interested in using the horoscope to cast light on complications in the character. He believed that the horoscope could help to overcome difficulties by giving a different viewpoint to the problems being addressed, and this might lead to a diagnosis.

Jung was most interested in the seasonal and planetary influences of the sun sign. He once said, "We are born at a given moment in a given place, and like vintage years of wine, we have the qualities of the year and of the season in which we are born. Astrology does not lay claim to anything else."

Jung's interest in astrology continues to be an embarrassment to many psychotherapists and may have caused his break with Freud. Nonetheless, Jung did a great deal of research into astrology and devised a number of statistical tests for a possible causal link between psychic states and real events. His investigations eventually led to the development of his important theory of synchronicity.

SIGNS, STORIES, EXPERIMENTS, AND SYMBOLS

In order to accurately plot a horoscope, you need an ephemeris and a table of houses. In the early 1950s, mathematicians at NASA and the Astrological Association of Great Britain were all working on a simple way to work out a table that would give the position of the moon from the year 1800 to the year 2000 in three simple steps. One of the astrologers involved was Hugh MacCraig. One evening as he lay down to sleep, MacCraig "prayed on it," and at 3:00 A.M., he awoke to discover that he had dreamed of the solution. The resulting mathematical table was published in 1952 in his book, *Ephemeris of the Moon*. It has become the model for the Ephemeris used by modern astrologers today.

 Bibliography

Bartlett, John, and Justin Kaplan. *Bartlett's Familiar Quotations*. London: Little Brown & Company, 2002.

Black Elk. *Black Elk Speaks: Being the Life Story of a Holy Man of the Oglala Sioux,* 21st-century edition. New York: Bison Books Corporation, 2000.

Blakemore, Colin. *Mechanics of the Mind*. Cambridge, England: Cambridge University Press, 1977.

Boa, F. *The Way of the Dream: Conversations on Jungian Dream Interpretation with Marie-Louise von Franz*. Boston: Shambhala, 1994.

Bulkeley, Kelly. *Transforming Dreams: Learning Spiritual Lessons from the Dreams You Never Forget*. John Wiley & Sons, 2000.

Capra, Fritjof. *The Tao of Physics*. Toronto: Bantam Books, 1988.

Castle, Kit and Stefan Bechtel. *Katherine, It's Time: An Incredible Journey into the World of a Multiple Personality*. New York: Harper & Row, 1989.

Chetwynd, Tom. *Dictionary of Symbols*. London: Thorsons, 1982.

Cleary, T., translator. *The Taoist I Ching*. Boston: Shambhala, 1986.

Cook, John. *The Book of Positive Quotations*. New York: Gramercy, 1999.

Crowley, A. *The Book of Thoth: A Short Essay on the Tarot of the Egyptians*. York Beach, Maine: Samuel Weiser, 1944/1985.

Davis, Jim. *In Dog Years I'd Be Dead: Garfield at 25*. New York: Ballantine Books, 2002.

Dass, Ram. *Journey of Awakening: A Meditator's Guide*. Bantam Books: New York, 1978.

Delaney, Gayle. *Living Your Dreams*. San Francisco: Harper, 1996.

Dingle, Carol A. *Memorable Quotations: Philosophers of Western Civilization*. Lincoln, Nebraska: Writer's Showcase Press, 2000.

Drury, Nevill. *The Elements of Human Potential*. Longmead, Dorset, England: Element Books, 1989.

Edwards, Sterling. *Alexis Carrel: Visionary Surgeon*. Springfield, Illinois: Charles C. Thomas, Publisher Ltd., 1974.

Ehrlich, Eugene H. *The International Thesaurus of Quotations*. London: HarperCollins, 1996.

Evans, Hilary. *Alternate States of Consciousness: Unself, Overself, and Superself*. Wellingborough, Northamptonshire, England: Aquarian Press, 1989.

Faraday, Ann. *Dream Power: The Use of Dreams in Everyday Life*. London: Pan, 1972.

Fitzhenry, Robert. *Chambers Book of Quotations*. Edinburgh: W & R Chambers Limited, 1986.

Gackenbach, Jayne. *Control Your Dreams.* New York: HarperCollins, 1989.

Garrett, Eileen J. *Many Voices.* New York: Putnam, 1968.

Garfield, Patricia. *Creative Dreaming: A Revolutionary Approach to Increased Self-Awareness.* Aylesbury, UK: Futura Publications, 1976.

Gawain, Shakti. *Creative Visualisation.* San Rafael, California: New World Library, 1978.

Gordon, Leah. *Voodoo: Charms and Rituals to Empower Your Life.* London: Parkgate Books, 2000.

Green, Celia Elizabeth. *Lucid Dreaming: The Paradox of Consciousness During Sleep.* London: Routledge, 1995.

Greene, Graham. *A Sort of Life.* London: Bodley Head, 1971.

Greene, Liz and Juliet Sharman-Burke. *The Mythic Journey.* New York: Fireside, 2000.

Gregory, Richard L. *The Oxford Companion to the Mind.* Oxford, UK: Oxford University Press, 1987.

Huxley, Aldous. *Collected Essays.* New York: Harper & Brothers, 1923.

Knowles, Elizabeth. *Oxford Book of Quotations.* Los Angeles: Getty Center for Education in the Arts, 1999.

Jung, C.G. *Analytical Psychology, Its Theory and Practice: The Tavistock Lectures.* New York: Vintage Books, 1968.

Jung, C.G. *The Archetypes and the Collective Unconscious.* Translated by R. F. C. Hull. Bollingen Series XX. The Collected Works of C.G. Jung, 9, Part 1. Princeton, New Jersey: Princeton University Press, 1959/1990.

Jung, C.G. *The Development of Personality: Papers on Child Psychology, Education, and Related Subjects.* Translated by R.F.C. Hull. Bollingen Series XX: The Collected Works of C.G. Jung, 17. Princeton, New Jersey: Princeton University Press, 1954/1991.

Jung, C.G. *Man and His Symbols.* Garden City, New York: Doubleday, 1964.

Jung, C.G. *Memories, Dreams, Reflections.* New York: Vintage Books, 1989.

Jung, C.G. *Mysterium Coniunctionis.* Translated by R.F.C. Hull. Bollingen Series XX. The Collected Works of C.G. Jung, 14. Princeton, New Jersey: Princeton University Press, 1963/1989.

Jung, C.G. *The Practice of Psychotherapy: Essays on the Psychology of the Transference and Other Subjects.* Translated by R.F.C. Hull. Bollingen Series XX. The Collected Works of C.G. Jung, 16. Princeton, New Jersey: Princeton University Press, 1954/1966.

Jung, C.G. *Symbols of Transformation.* Translated by R.F.C. Hull. Bollingen Series XX. The Collected Works of C.G. Jung, 5. Princeton, New Jersey: Princeton University Press, 1956/1976.

Kelzer, Kenneth. *The Sun and the Shadow: My Experiment with Lucid Dreaming.* Virginia Beach, Virginia: A.R.E. Press, 1987.

Laberge, Stephen. *Lucid Dreaming.* New York: Ballantine Books, 1998.

Laing, R. D. *The Politics of Experience.* New York: Random House, 1967.

Lilly, John C. *The Center of the Cyclone: An Autobiography of Inner Space.* New York: Julian Press, 1985.

Mansfield, Victor. *Synchronicity, Science and Soul-Making.* Chicago, Illinois: Open Court Publishing, 1995.

Moss, Robert. *Conscious Dreaming: A Spiritual Path for Everyday Life.* New York: Crown Publishing, 1996.

Novalis. *Fragmente, in Werke Briefe Dokumente.* Edited by E. Wasmuth. Heidelberg, Germany: Verlag Lambert Schneider, 1957.

Opie, Iona. *Oxford Dictionary of Superstitions.* Oxford, UK: Oxford University Press, 1989.

Pickering, David. *The Cassell Dictionary of Folklore.* London: Cassell, 1999.

Plaskett, James. *Coincidences.* London: Tamworth Press, 2000.

Robins, Stephen. *The Ruling Asses: A Little Book of Political Stupidity.* London: Prion Books, 2001.

Ryback, David. *Dreams that Come True.* New York: Doubleday, 1989.

Sacks, Oliver. *The Man Who Mistook His Wife for a Hat.* New York: Harper & Row, 1987.

Satchidananda, Swami. *Yoga Sutras of Patanjali.* Buckingham, Virginia: Integral Yoga Distribution, 1990.

Schucman, Helen, with Kenneth Wapnick. *A Course in Miracles: What It Says.* London: Penguin Audiobooks, 1996.

Sechrist, Elsie. *Dreams: Your Magic Mirror.* Virginia Beach, Virginia: A.R.E. Press, 1995.

Sherwood, S.J. "Relationship Between the Hypnagogic/Hypnopompic States and Reports of Anomalous Experiences." *Journal of Parapsychology.* Durham, North Carolina, 2002.

Taylor, Jeremy. *Where People Fly and Water Runs Uphill: Using Dreams to Tap the Wisdom of the Unconscious.* New York: Warner Books, 1993.

Tillich, Paul. *The Courage to Be.* New Haven, Connecticut: Yale University Press, 2000.

Tillich, Paul. *Morality and Beyond.* Louisville, Kentucky: Westminster John Knox Press, 1995.

Ullman, Montague, and Stanley Krippner. *Dream Studies and Telepathy.* New York: Parapsychology Foundation, 1970.

Von Franz, Marie-Louise. *On Dreams & Death.* Boston and London: Shambhala, 1987.

Wilhelm, Hellmut. *The I Ching or Book of Changes.* London: Routledge & Kegan Paul Ltd., 1951.

Wilson, Colin. *The Directory of Possibilities.* Devon, UK: Webb & Bower, 1981.

Wolf, Fred Alan. *The Dreaming Universe: A Mind-Expanding Journey into the Realm Where Psyche and Physics Meet.* Touchstone Books, 1995.

Young, Lailan. *Love Around the World.* Kent, UK: Hodder & Stoughton, 1985.

Index of Psychic Dream Meanings

Below is a list of dream themes that have been covered in this book. Look up the specific entry to discover the meaning of your psychic dream. The entry is marked in bold text in the appropriate section.

A

Abandon—*See:* Afterlife, Money

Abbess—*See:* Biblical Prophecies

Abbey—*See:* Biblical Prophecies, Buildings and Places, Money

Abbot—*See:* Biblical Prophecies

Abdomen—*See:* Luck

Abduct—*See:* Unidentified Flying Objects (UFOs)

Abroad—*See:* Journeys

Abundance—*See:* Oneiromancy

Abyss—*See:* Oneiromancy

Accident—*See:* Accidents, Introduction

Accountant—*See:* Money

Acorn—*See:* Money

Acrobat—*See:* People

Acting—*See:* Journeys

Adam and Eve—*See:* Biblical Prophecies

Adventure—*See:* Journeys

Advertisement—*See:* Telepathy

Air—*See:* Nature, Numerology, Oneiromancy

Airplane—*See:* Money

Alarm—*See:* Luck

Alchemist—*See:* Unidentified Flying Objects (UFOs)

Alien—*See:* People, Unidentified Flying Objects (UFOs)

Alligator—*See:* Animal Symbols, Luck

Altar—*See:* Biblical Prophecies

Altitude—*See:* Nature

Ambition—*See:* Oneiromancy

Ambulance—*See:* Luck

Amputation—*See:* Health and Healing

Anchor—*See:* Money

Angels—*See:* Xenoglossy

Anima—*See:* Death and Dying, Oracles, Soulmates

Animals—*See:* Animal Symbols, Death and Dying

Animus—*See:* Death and Dying, Oracles, Soulmates

Ankles—*See:* Health and Healing

Ant—*See:* Animal Symbols

Antiques—*See:* Money

Ape—*See:* Animal Symbols

Apocalypse—*See:* Disasters

Appreciation—*See:* Oneiromancy

Apron—*See:* Money

Arial—*See:* Money

Arm—*See:* Health and Healing

Artist—*See:* Luck

Ascending—*See:* Luck, Oneiromancy

Ash—*See:* Money, Spells

Atlas—*See:* Journeys

Attack—*See:* Afterlife, Hypnagogic and Hypnopompic Dreams

Attic—*See:* Buildings and Places

Audience—*See:* Symbolism

Author—*See:* Luck

B

Babies—*See:* Afterlife, Numinous Dreams, People

Bacchus—*See:* Luck

Back—*See:* Health and Healing

Bag—*See:* Journeys, Money

Baker—*See:* Luck

Baldness—*See:* Health and Healing

Bandages—*See:* Health and Healing

Bank—*See:* Oneiromancy

Baptism—*See:* Biblical Prophecies

Barber—*See:* Luck

Barbed wire—*See:* Telepathy

Barn—*See:* Oneiromancy

Barometer—*See:* Nature

Basement—*See:* Buildings and Places

Battle—*See:* Luck

Beans—*See:* Money

Bear—*See:* Animal Spirits

Beard—*See:* Health and Healing

Bedroom—*See:* Buildings and Places

Bees—*See:* Animal Symbols

Beetle—*See:* Animal Symbols, Coincidence and Synchronocity

Beggar—*See:* Luck

Bench—*See:* Luck

Berries—*See:* Luck

Betrayal—*See:* Work

Bible—*See:* Biblical Prophecies

Bicycle—*See:* Luck

Birds—*See:* Animal Symbols, Superstitions

Birth—*See:* Luck

Bishop—*See:* Biblical Prophecies, Luck

Blackbird—*See:* Animal Symbols

Blasphemy—*See:* Biblical Prophecies

Blemish—*See:* Health and Healing

Blindness—*See:* Health and Healing

Blood—*See:* Health and Healing

Blunder—*See:* Luck

Boat—*See:* Journeys

Boatman—*See:* Soulmates

Body—*See:* Health and Healing

Bolt—*See:* Oneiromancy

Bones—*See:* Health and Healing

Boss—*See:* Luck

Bowl—*See:* Oneiromancy

Bra—*See:* Telepathy

Bricks—*See:* Buildings and Places

Bride—*See:* People

Bridegroom—*See:* People

Bridge—*See:* Afterlife, Death and Dying, Journeys

Briefcase—*See:* Journeys, Luck

Bruise—*See:* Health and Healing

Bucket—*See:* Oneiromancy

Buffalo—*See:* Animal Spirits, Health and Healing

Bunion—*See:* Journeys

Burglar—*See:* Death and Dying, Luck

Burial—*See:* Death and Dying

Burning—*See:* Money

Bus—*See:* Journeys, Time

Butterfly—*See:* Animal Symbols

Button—*See:* Money

C

Cab—*See:* Journeys

Cabin—*See:* Journeys

Cage—*See:* Oneiromancy

Call—*See:* Luck

Camel—*See:* Health and Healing, Journeys

Canal—*See:* Oneiromancy

Candles—*See:* Time

Cannibalism—*See:* People

Canyon—*See:* Oneiromancy

Car Crash—*See:* Accidents, Introduction

Cargo—*See:* Journeys

Cars—*See:* Afterlife, Symbolism

Cart—*See:* Journeys

Castle—*See:* Buildings and Places

Cat—*See:* Animal Spirits, Animal Symbols, Health and Healing, Oriental Dreams

Catastrophe—*See:* Oracles

Cattle—*See:* Animal Symbols, Money

Cave—*See:* Oneiromancy

Celebration—*See:* Oneiromancy

Cellar—*See:* Buildings and Places, Oneiromancy

Cemetery—*See:* Buildings and Places

Chalice—*See:* Biblical Prophecies

Chariot—*See:* Journeys, Oracles

Chase—*See:* Lucid Dreams, Symbolism

Cheat—*See:* Afterlife

Cheese—*See:* Money

Children—*See:* Afterlife, Luck

Chimney—*See:* Luck

Christ—*See:* Biblical Prophecies, Oracles

Church—*See:* Biblical Prophecies, Buildings and Places

Circle—*See:* Wicca and Witchcraft

Circus—*See:* Buildings and Places

City—*See:* Telepathy

Cleaning—*See:* Luck

Cliff—*See:* Oneiromancy

Clock—*See:* Luck

Cloth—*See:* Health and Healing

Clothes—*See:* Health and Healing

Clouds—*See:* Nature, Oneiromancy

Coffee—*See:* Luck

Coffin—*See:* Death and Dying, Oriental Dreams

Coins—*See:* Money

Coldness—*See:* Afterlife

Colors—*See:* Mutual Dreams
Comet—*See:* Journeys,
  Superstitions
Committee—*See:* Luck
Computers—*See:* Symbolism
Concert—*See:* Oneiromancy
Contrary—*See:* Oneiromancy
Cooking—*See:* Money
Corpse—*See:* Death and
  Dying, Health and Healing
Cosmetics—*See:* Oriental
  Dreams
Cough—*See:* Health and
  Healing
Counterfeit—*See:* Money
Country—*See:* Telepathy
Courage—*See:* Oneiromancy
Court—*See:* Money
Cow—*See:* Animal Symbols,
  Oriental Dreams
Crime—*See:* Money
Criticism—*See:* Oneiromancy
Crocodile—*See:* Animal
  Symbols
Crone—*See:* Wicca and
  Witchcraft
Cross—*See:* Biblical Prophecies
Crutch—*See:* Oneiromancy
Crying—*See:* Oneiromancy
Cuckoo—*See:* Animal Symbols
Cup—*See:* Oneiromancy
Cushions—*See:* Luck

D
Dagger—*See:* Luck
Dam—*See:* Luck
Dawn—*See:* Luck
Death—*See:* Afterlife, Death
  and Dying, Health and
  Healing, Introduction,
  Luck, Oracles, Symbolism
Deer—*See:* Animal Spirits

Demons—*See:* Hypnagogic
  and Hypnopompic Dreams,
  Psychic Attack
Descending—*See:* Luck,
  Oneiromancy
Desert—*See:* Journeys
Devil—*See:* Intuition, Oracles,
  Wicca and Witchcraft
Dirty—*See:* Luck
Dish—*See:* Money
Ditch—*See:* Oneiromancy
Divorce—*See:* Afterlife
Doctor—*See:* Health and
  Healing
Dog—*See:* Animal Spirits,
  Animal Symbols, Death
  and Dying, Oriental
  Dreams, Superstition,
  Tribal Dream Interpretation
Doll—*See:* People
Dolphin—*See:* Animal Spirits
Door—*See:* Afterlife,
  Oneiromancy, Oriental
  Dreams
Dove—*See:* Death and Dying
Downhill—*See:* Oneiromancy
Dragon—*See:* Animal
  Symbols, Luck, Oriental
  Dreams
Drawbridge—*See:* Journeys
Drink—*See:* Oneiromancy
Driving—*See:* Journeys
Drowning—*See:* Health and
  Healing
Drugs—*See:* Health and
  Healing
Dull—*See:* Luck

E
Eagle—*See:* Animal Spirits,
  Animal Symbols
Earth—*See:* Luck, Numerology

Earwig—*See:* Luck
East—*See:* Journeys
Eclipse—*See:* Superstition
Elephant—*See:* Animal
  Symbols
E-mail—*See:* Telepathy
Embarrassment—*See:* Luck
Embezzlement—*See:* Money
Emigration—*See:* Journeys
Emperor—*See:* Oracles
Employment—*See:* Luck
Empress—*See:* Oracles
Entertainment—*See:*
  Oneiromancy
Entombment—*See:* Luck
Entrails—*See:* Money
Escalators—*See:* Oneiromancy
Escape—*See:* Luck
Eskimo—*See:* Money
Evergreens—*See:* Money
Examination—*See:*
  Oneiromancy, Symbolism
Explosion—*See:* Afterlife
Eyelashes—*See:* Health and
  Healing
Eyelids—*See:* Health and
  Healing
Eyes—*See:* Health and
  Healing

F
Faces—*See:* Health and
  Healing
Factory—*See:* Buildings and
  Places, Luck
Family—*See:* Luck
Failure—*See:* Luck
Fall—*See:* Nature
Falling—*See:* Oneiromancy,
  Symbolism
Famous people—*See:* Health
  and Healing, Luck

Farewell—*See:* Journeys
Farm—*See:* Buildings and Places, Oneiromancy
Father—*See:* Oracles
Fear—*See:* Afterlife, Oneiromancy
Feathers—*See:* Luck
Feet—*See:* Health and Healing, Journeys
Fence—*See:* Afterlife, Oneiromancy
Ferret—*See:* Luck
Field—*See:* Journeys, Oneiromancy
Film—*See:* Oneiromancy
Fire—*See:* Death and Dying, Numerology
Fish—*See:* Animal Symbols, Money
Flag—*See:* Luck
Flamingo—*See:* Journeys
Flatulence—*See:* Journeys, Luck
Flies—*See:* Animal Symbols
Floating—*See:* Money
Flood—*See:* Oneiromancy
Floor—*See:* Luck
Flowers—*See:* Death and Dying
Flying—*See:* Journeys, Lucid Dreaming, Out-of-Body Experiences, Symbolism
Food—*See:* Health and Healing, Money
Fool—*See:* Oracles
Footsteps—*See:* Luck
Forecast—*See:* Nature
Foreign countries—*See:* Xenoglossy
Foreign language—*See:* Xenoglossy

Foreigners—*See:* Xenoglossy
Fountain—*See:* Soulmates
Fox—*See:* Animal Symbols, Health and Healing
Friday—*See:* Omens
Frost—*See:* Nature
Fruit—*See:* Health and Healing
Funeral—*See:* Death and Dying
Furniture—*See:* Luck

G

Gain—*See:* Oneiromancy
Gallows—*See:* Buildings and Places
Gambling—*See:* Money
Gangway—*See:* Luck
Garden—*See:* Afterlife, Oneiromancy
Gate—*See:* Afterlife
Garnet—*See:* Luck
Gate—*See:* Oneiromancy
Ghost—*See:* Afterlife, Oneiromancy
Gifts—*See:* Health and Healing
Giggling—*See:* Money
Glass—*See:* Oneiromancy
Gloom—*See:* Nature
Gloves—*See:* Luck
Goat—*See:* Animal Symbols
Gold—*See:* Money
Gold mine—*See:* Buildings and Places
Gondola—*See:* Journeys
Gondolier—*See:* People
Government buildings—*See:* Buildings and Places
Graffiti—*See:* Telepathy
Grass—*See:* Afterlife

Green man—*See:* Death and Dying
Greenhouse—*See:* Buildings and Places
Grotto—*See:* Journeys
Guard—*See:* Luck
Guide—*See:* Guides and Gurus
Gun—*See:* Luck
Guru—*See:* Guides and Gurus, Unidentified Flying Objects (UFOs)
Gypsy—*See:* People

H

Hail—*See:* Nature
Hammer—*See:* Luck
Hand—*See:* Health and Healing
Handcuff—*See:* Luck, Oneiromancy
Hanged Man—*See:* Oracles
Hanging—*See:* Afterlife
Happiness—*See:* Oneiromancy, Oracles
Harem—*See:* Buildings and Places
Harvest—*See:* Oneiromancy
Haunted houses—*See:* Afterlife
Hay—*See:* Money
Head—*See:* Journeys
Hearse—*See:* Luck
Heaven—*See:* Nature
Hedge—*See:* Oneiromancy
Helmet—*See:* Luck
Helplessness—*See:* Afterlife
Hermit—*See:* Oracles
Hero—*See:* Afterlife, Oracles
Hiccups—*See:* Journeys
Hiding—*See:* Luck
Hierophant—*See:* Oracles

Hills—*See:* Buildings and Places, Journeys, Oneiromancy

Hive—*See:* Luck

Hoarding—*See:* Money

Hoax—*See:* Luck

Holiday—*See:* Buildings and Places

Holly—*See:* Luck

Holy buildings—*See:* Biblical Prophecies

Holy communion—*See:* Biblical Prophecies

Holy people—*See:* Health and Healing

Horns—*See:* Oriental Dreams

Horse—*See:* Animal Spirits, Animal Symbols, Health and Healing, Luck

Hospital—*See:* Health and Healing

Hotel—*See:* Buildings and Places

House—*See:* Buildings and Places

Hummingbird—*See:* Journeys

Hunger—*See:* Luck

Hunting—*See:* Afterlife

Hymns—*See:* Biblical Prophecies

I

Ice—*See:* Afterlife, Luck, Nature

Iceberg—*See:* Buildings and Places

Illness—*See:* Health and Healing

Income—*See:* Luck, Money

Incubus—*See:* Psychic Attacks

Inferiority—*See:* Oneiromancy

Injury—*See:* Health and Healing

Inn—*See:* Buildings and Places

Insects—*See:* Animal Symbols

Invalid—*See:* Health and Healing

Invitation—*See:* Money

Island—*See:* Buildings and Places, Journeys

Itch—*See:* Health and Healing

Ivy—*See:* Money

J

Jackdaw—*See:* Animal Symbols

Jail—*See:* Buildings and Places, Journeys

Javelin—*See:* Luck

Jetty—*See:* Journeys

Job—*See:* Luck

Journey—*See:* Death and Dying, Journeys

Judge—*See:* People

Judgment—*See:* Oracles

Jug—*See:* Journeys

Juggler—*See:* People

Jumping—*See:* Lucid Dreams

Jungle—*See:* Money

Justice—*See:* Oracles

K

Kangaroo—*See:* Animal Symbols

Kettle—*See:* Money

Killing—*See:* Afterlife

Kilt—*See:* Journeys

Knapsack—*See:* Journeys

Knee—*See:* Telepathy

Knife—*See:* Luck

Knight—*See:* People

Knives—*See:* Oneiromancy

L

Labyrinth—*See:* Oneiromancy

Lace—*See:* Money

Ladders—*See:* Oneiromancy

Lake—*See:* Health and Healing

Landing—*See:* Journeys

Landscape—*See:* Afterlife, Lucid Dreams, Oneiromancy

Lavatory—*See:* Luck

Lawyer—*See:* People

Leaping—*See:* Lucid Dreams

Letter—*See:* Oneiromancy, Telepathy

Libraries—*See:* Buildings and Places

Lifeboat—*See:* Journeys

Lighthouse—*See:* Journeys

Lightning—*See:* Afterlife, Nature, Parapsychology

Limping—*See:* Journeys

Lion—*See:* Animal Spirits, Animal Symbols, Luck

Lizard—*See:* Animal Symbols

Lobster—*See:* Animal Symbols

Lock—*See:* Afterlife, Oneiromancy

Log—*See:* Money

Loss—*See:* Oneiromancy

Lost—*See:* Afterlife

Lotus—*See:* Death and Dying

Lovers—*See:* Oracles

Lunatic—*See:* Luck

M

Machinery—*See:* Luck

Magic circle—*See:* Unidentified Flying Objects (UFOs)

Magician—*See:* Oracles

Magnet—*See:* Luck

Magpie—*See:* Animal Symbols

Maiden—*See:* Wicca and Witchcraft

Mandala—*See:* Oracles, Unidentified Flying Objects (UFOs)

Map—*See:* Journeys

Market—*See:* Oneiromancy

Marsh—*See:* Journeys

Meat—*See:* Money

Medium—*See:* Luck

Messenger—*See:* People

Mice—*See:* Animal Symbols

Microphone—*See:* Telepathy

Midnight—*See:* Time

Mill—*See:* Luck

Mirage—*See:* Nature

Mischievous Spirits—*See:* Psychic Attacks

Mist—*See:* Nature

Money—*See:* Money

Monk—*See:* Biblical Prophecies

Monkey—*See:* Animal Symbols, Health and Healing

Monster—*See:* Afterlife

Moon—*See:* Oracles, Wicca and Witchcraft

Mother—*See:* Oracles, Wicca and Witchcraft

Mountain—*See:* Health and Healing, Oneiromancy

Mouth—*See:* Health and Healing

Mud—*See:* Afterlife

Murder—*See:* Afterlife

N

Name—*See:* Oriental Dreams

Napkin—*See:* Luck

Navigation—*See:* Journeys

Navy—*See:* Journeys

Neck—*See:* Health and Healing

Needle—*See:* Money

Nest—*See:* Money

Newt—*See:* Animal Symbols

Night—*See:* Afterlife

Noon—*See:* Time

Nose—*See:* Health and Healing

Nudity—*See:* Afterlife, Luck, Symbolism

Numbers—*See:* Numerology

Nun—*See:* Biblical Prophecies

Nurse—*See:* Health and Healing

O

Obstacles—*See:* Oneiromancy

Ocean—*See:* Journeys

Office—*See:* Buildings and Places, Luck

Onion—*See:* Money

Orders—*See:* Luck

Orient—*See:* Journeys

Owl—*See:* Animal Spirits, Animal Symbols, Money, Superstition

Ox—*See:* Animal Symbols

P

Packing—*See:* Journeys

Pan—*See:* Wicca and Witchcraft

Paralysis—*See:* Health and Healing, Paralysis

Parents—*See:* People

Park—*See:* Buildings and Places

Parrot—*See:* Animal Symbols

Party—*See:* Buildings and Places

Passage—*See:* Afterlife

Path—*See:* Oneiromancy

Peace—*See:* Oneiromancy

Pearls—*See:* Money, Oriental Dreams

Pendulum—*See:* Journeys, Luck

Penis—*See:* Oneiromancy

Perjury—*See:* Money

Phoenix—*See:* Afterlife, Oriental Dreams

Pig—*See:* Animal Symbols, Luck, Oriental Dreams

Pigeons—*See:* Animal Symbols, Telepathy

Pilgrims—*See:* Biblical Prophecies, Journeys

Pirate—*See:* Journeys

Plant—*See:* Oneiromancy

Play—*See:* Oneiromancy

Poverty—*See:* Oneiromancy

Pregnant—*See:* Oriental Dreams

Priestess—*See:* Oracles

Princess Diana—*See:* Disasters

Prison—*See:* Oneiromancy

Prize—*See:* Luck

Punishing—*See:* Afterlife

Puns—*See:* Telepathy

Puppets—*See:* Luck

Pyramid—*See:* Buildings and Places

Pyramids—*See:* Time

Q

Quail—*See:* Animal Symbols, Journeys

Quaker—*See:* Biblical Prophecies

Quarrel—*See:* Luck

Quarry—*See:* Buildings and Places

Quartz—*See:* Money
Question—*See:* Oneiromancy
Quicksand—*See:* Buildings and Places
Quilt—*See:* Money

R

Rabbit—*See:* Animal Spirits, Animal Symbols, Money
Racecourse—*See:* Buildings and Places
Radio—*See:* Telepathy
Raffle—*See:* Money
Raft—*See:* Journeys, Luck
Rain—*See:* Nature, Oriental Dreams
Rainbow—*See:* Journeys, Nature
Rape—*See:* Afterlife
Raspberry—*See:* Journeys
Rat—*See:* Animal Symbols
Rebirth—*See:* Afterlife, Oracles
Regrets—*See:* Oneiromancy
Religious figures—*See:* Biblical Prophecies
Rescue—*See:* Journeys
Restaurant—*See:* Buildings and Places
Rest room—*See:* Luck
Rivalry—*See:* Oneiromancy
River—*See:* Soulmates
Road—*See:* Afterlife, Journeys
Rock—*See:* Oneiromancy
Rooster—*See:* Oriental Dreams
Ropes—*See:* Oneiromancy
Rudder—*See:* Journeys
Running—*See:* Afterlife, Lucid Dreams

S

Sage—*See:* Unidentified Flying Objects (UFOs)
Sailing—*See:* Journeys
Salamander—*See:* Afterlife
Salt—*See:* Money, Superstition
Sand—*See:* Money
Satan—*See:* Biblical Prophecies, Psychic Attacks
Saturday—*See:* Omens
Scarab—*See:* Coincidences
School—*See:* Buildings and Places
Scissors—*See:* Oneiromancy
Self-sacrifice—*See:* Oracles
Serpent—*See:* Oneiromancy, Time
Setbacks—*See:* Oneiromancy
Shadow—*See:* Afterlife
Sharing—*See:* Money
Sharp—*See:* Oneiromancy
Shaving—*See:* Journeys, Oriental Dreams
Sheep—*See:* Journeys
Shiny—*See:* Luck
Shipwreck—*See:* Journeys
Shower—*See:* Nature
Signature—*See:* Luck
Silk—*See:* Oriental Dreams
Silver—*See:* Money
Singing—*See:* Oriental Dreams
Sky—*See:* Nature
Sky god—*See:* Unidentified Flying Objects (UFOs)
Smell—*See:* Oneiromancy
Snakes—*See:* Afterlife, Animal Symbols, Oneiromancy, Oriental Dreams, Symbolism
Snow—*See:* Luck
Soulmate—*See:* Mutual Dreams, Soulmates
Spider—*See:* Animal Symbols, Oriental Dreams

Spirits—*See:* Afterlife
Spring—*See:* Soulmates
Stabbed—*See:* Work
Stairs—*See:* Accidents, Oneiromancy
Standing Stones—*See:* Time
Star—*See:* Journeys, Oracles, Oriental Dreams
Steeple—*See:* Biblical Prophecies
Strangers—*See:* People
Street—*See:* Oneiromancy
Strength—*See:* Oracles
Striding—*See:* Lucid Dreaming
Success—*See:* Luck
Struggle—*See:* Oneiromancy
Succubus—*See:* Psychic Attacks
Suicide—*See:* Afterlife
Summer—*See:* Nature
Sun—*See:* Afterlife, Nature, Oracles
Sundial—*See:* Nature, Time
Superhuman—*See:* Lucid Dreams
Superiority—*See:* Oneiromancy
Swamps—*See:* Money
Swimming—*See:* Money
Sword—*See:* Oneiromancy

T

Table—*See:* Luck
Teacher—*See:* People
Teeth—*See:* Health and Healing, Oriental Dreams, Symbolism
Telephone—*See:* Money, Telepathy
Television—*See:* Oneiromancy
Temperance—*See:* Oracles

Tempest—*See:* Nature
Thermometer—*See:* Nature
Thief—*See:* Afterlife
Thighs—*See:* Journeys
Thunder—*See:* Nature
Thunderbolt—*See:* Nature
Tiger—*See:* Animal Symbols, Health and Healing, Oriental Dreams
Till—*See:* Money
Time—*See:* Afterlife, Time
Toad—*See:* Animal Symbols, Money
Toe—*See:* Telepathy
Tomb—*See:* Oriental Dreams
Tools—*See:* Money
Tornado—*See:* Nature
Torture—*See:* Afterlife
Towel—*See:* Luck
Tower—*See:* Oneiromancy, Oracles, Parapsychology
Traffic—*See:* Oneiromancy
Train—*See:* Journeys
Trees—*See:* Death and Dying, Health and Healing
Trinity—*See:* Biblical Prophecies
Trouble—*See:* Oneiromancy
Trumpet—*See:* Money
Tunnel—*See:* Buildings and Places
Turtles—*See:* Oriental Dreams
Twins—*See:* Money

U

Umbrella—*See:* Money
Unicorn—*See:* Luck
Uniform—*See:* Luck

V

Valley—*See:* Journeys, Oneiromancy

Vatican—*See:* Biblical Prophecies
Vegetables—*See:* Money
Vegetation—*See:* Death and Dying
Vehicle—*See:* Oriental Dreams
Vest—*See:* Luck
Vicar—*See:* Biblical Prophecies
View—*See:* Journeys
Violence—*See:* Afterlife, Oracles
Virgins—*See:* Oracles
Visitor—*See:* People
Volcano—*See:* Buildings and Places
Voyage—*See:* Journeys
Vulture—*See:* Animal Symbols

W

Wages—*See:* Luck, Money
Waiter—*See:* People
Walking—*See:* Lucid Dreams
Wall—*See:* Afterlife, Oneiromancy
Wallet—*See:* Oneiromancy
Wandering—*See:* Journeys
War—*See:* Afterlife
Water—*See:* Afterlife, Death and Dying, Numerology, Oneiromancy, Oriental Dreams
Wayfarer—*See:* Journeys
Wealth—*See:* Money, Oneiromancy
Weather—*See:* Nature, Oneiromancy
Wedding—*See:* Death and Dying
Well—*See:* Oriental Dreams
West—*See:* Death and Dying
Wheel—*See:* Journeys, Oracles

Widower—*See:* People
Wind—*See:* Nature, Oneiromancy
Winter—*See:* Nature
Wise person—*See:* Oracles, Unidentified Flying Objects (UFOs)
Witch—*See:* Unidentified Flying Objects (UFOs), Wicca and Witchcraft
Wizard—*See:* People, Unidentified Flying Objects (UFOs), Wicca and Witchcraft
Wolf—*See:* Animal Spirits, Death and Dying
Womb—*See:* Afterlife
Wool—*See:* Luck
Words—*See:* Xenoglossy
World—*See:* Oracles
Worm—*See:* Animal Symbols, Time
Writing—*See:* Money

X

X ray—Health and Healing

Y

Yacht—*See:* Journeys

Z

Zebra—*See:* Animal Symbols
Zeppelin—*See:* Luck
Zinc—*See:* Luck
Zodiac—*See:* Zodiac
Zombies—*See:* Afterlife
Zoo—*See:* Buildings and Places, Journeys, Oneiromancy
Zulu—*See:* People

About the Author

Craig Hamilton-Parker is a celebrated British medium who has confounded skeptics with the uncanny accuracy of his readings. Craig and his wife, Jane, have demonstrated mediumship over the media to millions of television viewers worldwide. Hamilton-Parker also writes articles and columns about psychic and mediumistic phenomena for national newspapers and magazines in England, Scotland, Ireland, South Africa, and Australia. His Web site (www.psychics.co.uk) has a community of mediums that meet in its chat rooms for regular debate and practice. It also has further details of the cases quoted here and other documented cases of mediumship. Readers are invited to visit the Web site to discuss this book and the author's other books published by Sterling.

Author photo © Craig Hamilton-Parker

Sterling Books by the same author:

The Psychic Casebook
The Hidden Meaning of Dreams
Remembering Your Dreams
What to Do When You Are Dead
Fantasy Dreaming
Unlock Your Secret Dreams
Protecting the Soul